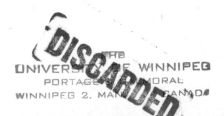

NIETZSCHE'S IMPACT

ON

MODERN GERMAN LITERATURE

UNIVERSITY OF NORTH CAROLINA
STUDIES IN THE GERMANIC LANGUAGES
AND LITERATURES

Initiated by RICHARD JENTE (1949–1952), *established by* F. E. COENEN (1952–1968)

Publication Committee

SIEGFRIED MEWS, EDITOR JOHN G. KUNSTMANN GEORGE S. LANE

HERBERT W. REICHERT CHRISTOPH E. SCHWEITZER SIDNEY R. SMITH

For other volumes in the "Studies" see pages 127 ff.

Send orders to: (U.S. and Canada)
The University of North Carolina Press, P.O. Box 2288
Chapel Hill, N.C. 27514
(All other countries) Feffer and Simons, Inc., 31 Union Square, New York, N.Y. 10003

NUMBER EIGHTY-FOUR

UNIVERSITY
OF NORTH CAROLINA
STUDIES IN
THE GERMANIC LANGUAGES
AND LITERATURES

Friedrich Nietzsche's Impact
on
Modern German Literature

Five Essays
by
Herbert W. Reichert

CHAPEL HILL
THE UNIVERSITY OF NORTH CAROLINA PRESS
1975

Library of Congress Cataloging in Publication Data

Reichert, Herbert William, 1917-
 Friedrich Nietzsche's impact on modern German literature.

 (University of North Carolina studies in the Germanic languages
and literatures; no. 84)
 "The writings of Herbert W. Reichert": pp. 117–26.
 1. Nietzsche, Friedrich Wilhelm, 1844–1900—Influence. 2. German literature—20th century—History and criticism. I. Title.
II. Series: North Carolina. University. Studies in the Germanic
languages and literatures; no. 84.

PT2440.N72Z79   193   75-5995
ISBN 0-8078-8084-1

Manufactured in the U.S.A.

Contents

A Tribute to Herbert W. Reichert

When in the fall of 1974 it became increasingly clear that Herbert W. Reichert's health was rapidly deteriorating and that he would not be physically able to carry on either his teaching duties or his scholarly activities in the spring of 1975, his colleagues and friends began to explore ways of honoring him for his many contributions to both the field of Germanics and the Department of Germanic Languages at Chapel Hill. Fortunately, Professor Reichert, who was unaware that some of his colleagues were pondering a *Festschrift* in his honor, indicated his wish to issue in book form some of his previously published essays dealing with Nietzsche's influence on five modern German authors. As he realized, time would not permit him to carry out his original design of completing a comprehensive study of Nietzsche's impact on all the major modern German authors.

These five essays then, although originally intended as building blocks for an edifice that must now remain unfinished, form the core of the present *Festschrift*. In their essentially unaltered form—editorial revisions and emendations have been kept to a minimum—Professor Reichert's essays reflect both his concentration on one area of research and his critical acumen in the application of one single methodological approach. Anyone familiar with Herbert Reichert's research with regard to Nietzsche knows that he did not confine himself to interpretive studies; in fact, he had to engage in some pioneering and laborious spade-work, which resulted in the *International Nietzsche Bibliography* (1st ed. 1960; co-editor Karl Schlechta), before he could begin formulating his influence studies. His endeavors were duly recognized when he was named the American representative of the German Nietzsche Society in 1957 and, one year later, was awarded a Guggenheim Fellowship which enabled him to continue his research on Nietzsche.

The appended bibliography of Herbert W. Reichert's writings attests to his wide range of interest. Indeed, his contributions are so numerous that only a very few can be mentioned here. There are two authors who, next to Nietzsche, attracted Professor Reichert's special attention. His interest in the Austrian dramatist Arthur Schnitzler led to his affiliation with the International Arthur Schnitzler Research Association, an organization which he served as Vice President. But the writer who first stimulated his intellectual curiosity and who continued to occupy him was the Swiss poet and novelist Gottfried Keller.

In 1949, two years after Herbert Reichert had come to Chapel Hill as an Assistant Professor, his *Basic Concepts in the Philosophy of Gottfried Keller* was published as volume 1 of the "University of North Carolina Studies in the Germanic Languages and Literatures." It is only appropriate that now, more than 25 years and 80 volumes later, a book honoring Professor Reichert should appear in the same monograph series which he helped initiate and to which he gave his unstinting support both as a member of the Publication Committee and as chairman of the Department.

Even a cursory survey of Herbert Reichert's scholarly achievements would not be complete without mentioning his pedagogical endeavors. His desire to promote the study of German and to enrich and supplement the academic curriculum is evident from his editions of readers for advanced students, articles on pedagogy, the direction of plays in German, the presentation of courses in German on television, and the enlivening of *Oktoberfeste* and similar departmental festivities with accordion music. It came hardly as a surprise that, in recognition of his outstanding contributions to the teaching of German, Herbert Reichert was elected national President of Delta Phi Alpha and, in 1970, became a permanent honorary member of that organization.

In honoring the scholar and teacher one should not overlook those traits of Herbert Reichert which endear him to his students, colleagues, and friends. As a man who refused to be confined to the ivory tower of academia, he participated in life to the fullest extent. As a vigorous and enthusiastic outdoorsman he excelled in competitive sailing, enjoyed skiing with his family, and occasionally taught students and colleagues—often many years his juniors—a healthy lesson in tennis. The same *joie de vivre* or, more appropriately, *Lebensfreude* may be gleaned from Herbert Reichert's translations and adaptations of "ribald" tales for popular magazines—a pursuit in which he forsook the well-trodden paths of scholarly writing in favor of more unconventional modes of expression.

In dedicating this volume to Herbert W. Reichert we pay tribute to a colleague and friend, who, as a man, a teacher, and a scholar has so richly contributed to the life of the profession in general and to the growth of this Department in particular.

Chapel Hill, N. C. Siegfried Mews, Editor, UNCSGL&L
February 1975 Christoph E. Schweitzer
Sidney R. Smith

Tabula Gratulatoria

Walter Arndt
Dartmouth College
Hanover, New Hampshire

Armin Arnold
McGill University
Montreal, Canada

Anne F. Baecker
University of North Carolina
Greensboro

Max Lorenz Baeumer
University of Wisconsin
Madison

Judy Bartenstein
University of North Carolina
Chapel Hill

Kurt Bergel
Chapman College
Orange, California

Harry Bergholz
University of North Carolina
Chapel Hill

Jeffrey B. Berlin
State University of New York
Binghamton

Norman H. Binger
University of Kentucky
Lexington

Hermann Boeschenstein
McGill University
Montreal, Canada

Elizabeth E. Bohning
University of Delaware
Newark

Frank L. Borchardt
Duke University
Durham, North Carolina

Joseph E. Bourgeois
Xavier University
Cincinnati, Ohio

Wilhelm Braun
University of Rochester
Rochester, New York

George C. Buck
University of Washington
Seattle

Emmi Colton
University of North Carolina
Chapel Hill

Horst S. Daemmrich
Wayne State University
Detroit, Michigan

Willard Ticknor Daetsch
Ithaca College
Ithaca, New York

W. Grant Dahlstrom
University of North Carolina
Chapel Hill

Donald George Daviau
University of California
Riverside

Barbara Eger
University of North Carolina
Chapel Hill

William Eickhorst
Unicoi High School
Erwin, Tennessee

Graydon L. Ekdahl
University of North Carolina
Chapel Hill

Raymond A. English
University of North Carolina
Chapel Hill

Hansford M. Epes, Jr.
Davidson College
Davidson, North Carolina

Joerg and Renate Fichte
University of Denver
Denver, Colorado

Walter Karl Francke
University of North Carolina
Chapel Hill

Ralph S. Fraser
Wake Forest University
Winston-Salem, North Carolina

Horst Frenz
Indiana University
Bloomington

Werner P. Friederich
University of North Carolina
Chapel Hill

Norbert Fuerst
Indiana University
Bloomington

Alice Carol Gaar
Auburn University
Auburn, Alabama

Robert and Valerie Greenberg
University of North Carolina
Chapel Hill

Reinhold Grimm
University of Wisconsin
Madison

Doris Starr Guilloton
New York University
New York

Donald P. Haase
University of North Carolina
Chapel Hill

James Hardin
University of South Carolina
Columbia

Diether H. Haenicke
Wayne State University
Detroit, Michigan

Erich Heller
Northwestern University
Evanston, Illinois

Robert M. Helm
Wake Forest University
Winston-Salem, North Carolina

Gerd Hillen
University of California
Berkeley

Sarah Belinda Horton
University of North Carolina
Chapel Hill

Agnes Hostettler
Queens College
Charlotte, North Carolina

Adrian Hsia
McGill University
Montreal, Canada

Gerda G. Hurow
University of North Carolina
Chapel Hill

Sidney M. Johnson
Indiana University
Bloomington

Otto W. Johnston
University of Florida
Gainesville

Calvin N. Jones
University of North Carolina
Chapel Hill

Alexander Kallos
College of William and Mary
Williamsburg, Virginia

John Esten Keller
University of Kentucky
Lexington

Günter F. Klabes
Vassar College
Poughkeepsie, New York

Helmut Koopmann
Universität Augsburg
Germany

John G. Kunstmann
University of North Carolina
Chapel Hill

Albert L. Lancaster
Virginia Military Institute
Lexington

George S. Lane
University of North Carolina
Chapel Hill

Richard H. Lawson
San Diego State University
San Diego, California

Donald J. Lineback
Hollins College
Hollins College, Virginia

Wolfgang Lockemann
Hamline University
Garnett, Kansas

Gerwin Marahrens
University of Alberta
Edmonton, Canada

William Harold McClain
The Johns Hopkins University
Baltimore, Maryland

Volker Meid
University of Massachusetts
Amherst

Siegfried Mews
University of North Carolina
Chapel Hill

Joseph Mileck
University of California
Berkeley

P. M. Mitchell
University of Illinois
Urbana

Walter J. Mueller
University of Alaska
Fairbanks

Charles Murin
University of Montreal
Montreal, Canada

Helen M. Mustard
Columbia University
New York

James Carneal O'Flaherty
Wake Forest University
Winston-Salem, North Carolina

Wolfgang Paulsen
University of Massachusetts
Amherst

Herbert Penzl
University of California
Berkeley

Virginia Fan Price
University of North Carolina
Chapel Hill

Richard M. Reiten
University of North Carolina
Chapel Hill

Henry H. H. Remak
Indiana University
Bloomington

Linda Ruth Revis
University of North Carolina
Chapel Hill

William H. Rey
University of Washington
Seattle

Cambron Leigh Rice
University of North Carolina
Chapel Hill

Walter L. Robinson
Western Washington State College
Bellingham

Lutz Röhrich
Universität Freiburg
Germany

Hans-Gert Roloff
Technische Universität Berlin
Germany

Jörg Salaquarda
Freie Universität Berlin
Germany

Herman and Marion Salinger
Duke University
Durham, North Carolina

Wilmer D. Sanders
Wake Forest University
Winston-Salem, North Carolina

Marvin and Roslyn Schindler
Wayne State University
Detroit, Michigan

Ulrich Emil Schönenberger
University of North Carolina
Chapel Hill

George C. Schoolfield
Yale University
New Haven, Connecticut

Hans Joachim Schrimpf
Ruhr-Universität Bochum
Germany

Adolf E. Schroeder
University of Missouri
Columbia

Ernst Schürer
University of Florida
Gainesville

Christoph E. Schweitzer
University of North Carolina
Chapel Hill

Ingo Seidler
University of Michigan
Ann Arbor

Lester W. J. Seifert
University of Wisconsin
Madison

Timothy Frederick Sellner
Wake Forest University
Winston-Salem, North Carolina

Richard K. Seymour
University of Hawaii
Honolulu

Walter Silz
Columbia University
New York

Sofus Emmelov Simonsen
North Carolina State University
Raleigh

Thomas F. Skinner
Hermann Lietz-Schule
Haunetal, Germany

Richard A. Smith
University of North Carolina
Chapel Hill

Sidney R. Smith
University of North Carolina
Chapel Hill

Rainulf A. Stelzmann
University of South Florida
Tampa

Albrecht B. Strauss
University of North Carolina
Chapel Hill

Wolfgang Friedrich Wilhelm Taraba
University of Minnesota
Minneapolis

David S. Thatcher
University of Victoria
Victoria, Canada

Gerhart Tracy Waldorf
University of North Carolina
Chapel Hill

Adolph H. Wegener
Muhlenberg College
Allentown, Pennsylvania

A. Leslie Willson
University of Texas
Austin

Dorothy M. Ziegler
Summit, New Jersey

Department of Germanic Languages
University of Alberta
Edmonton, Canada

Germanistisches Institut
Ruhr-Universität Bochum
Bochum-Querenburg, Germany

Department of German
Bowdoin College
Brunswick, Maine

The General Library
University of California
Berkeley

Carleton College
Northfield, Minnesota

Department of Romance and Germanic Languages and Literatures
University of Cincinnati
Cincinnati, Ohio

Department of Foreign Languages and Literatures
East Carolina University
Greenville, North Carolina

Department of Germanic and Slavic Languages and Literatures
University of Florida
Gainesville

Gettysburg College Library
Gettysburg, Pennsylvania

Hollins College
Hollins College, Virginia

Seminar Library, Germanic Languages
Indiana University
Bloomington

Department of Germanic and Slavic Languages and Literatures
Kent State University
Kent, Ohio

Department of Germanic Languages and Literatures
University of Kentucky
Lexington

Department of Germanic and Slavic Languages
State University of New York
Buffalo

Department of Germanic Languages and Literatures
University of North Carolina
Chapel Hill

Foreign Languages Department
Principia College
Elsah, Illinois

Department of Modern Languages and Literatures
Swarthmore College
Swarthmore, Pennsylvania

Department of Germanic Languages
University of Virginia
Charlottesville

Wake Forest Library
Wake Forest University
Winston-Salem, North Carolina

Department of Romance and Germanic Languages and Literatures
Wayne State University
Detroit, Michigan

Western Michigan University Library
Western Michigan University
Kalamazoo

Department of German
University of Wisconsin
Madison

The College of Wooster Library
Wooster College
Wooster, Ohio

Acknowledgments

The author and the editor wish to thank the publishers and/or editors who gave their permission to reprint the following, previously published essays:

1. "Nietzsche's *Geniemoral* and Schnitzler's Ethics," a revised version of "The Ethical Import of the Artist in the works of Arthur Schnitzler," *Modern Austrian Literature*, 6/1–2 (1973), 123–50.
2. "Nietzsche und Carl Sternheim," *Nietzsche Studien*, 1 (1972), 334–52.
3. "Nietzsche and Georg Kaiser," *Studies in Philology*, 61 (1964), 85–108.
4. "Nietzschean Influence in *Der Mann ohne Eigenschaften*," *German Quarterly*, 39 (1966), 12–29.
5. *The Impact of Nietzsche on Hermann Hesse*. Mount Pleasant, Michigan: The Enigma Press, 1972.

Further, the financial assistance of the University Research Council of the University of North Carolina at Chapel Hill—which subsidized publication of this volume—is hereby gratefully acknowledged.

To
my wife Irene
and
daughter Susan

Introduction

When I first determined to write this book over twenty years ago, my intent was to provide a comprehensive presentation of Nietzsche's impact on modern German literature. I realized, of course, that the subject chosen would transcend the limits of any book-length study, would indeed transcend the capabilities of any single scholar. But I felt that if the project became the main endeavor of my academic career, the ultimate product of my effort might well be worthwhile.

My initial focus was directed toward those literary giants, Thomas and Heinrich Mann, both of whom were powerfully stimulated by Nietzsche. And, as the months and years passed, I began to accumulate significant data on other writers including Christian Morgenstern, Paul Ernst, Frank Wedekind, Hermann Broch, Gerhart Hauptmann, Stefan George, Richard Dehmel, Reinhard Sorge, Ernst Jünger, Ernst Wiechert, Hugo von Hofmannsthal, and Rainer Maria Rilke. I was happy with the progress I was making.

At the same time, it became increasingly clear to me that the book was going to take longer than anticipated. The reasons were these. First of all, I soon discovered that impact studies tend to involve a considerable amount of reading, not only of the published works, but also of the unpublished materials and correspondence of a given author. Then it developed that some of my most stimulating research, particularly that pertaining to Thomas and Heinrich Mann, never came to a satisfactory resolution; because the source material was almost limitless, I was continually tempted to probe further and more deeply. Lastly, the absence of, and obvious need for, an adequate Nietzsche bibliography led me to enter into the time-consuming task of editing with Karl Schlechta *The International Nietzsche Bibliography*, which has also become a continuing project.[1]

---

[1] *The International Nietzsche Bibliography* (Chapel Hill: The University of North Carolina Press, 1960; Rev. and expanded ed., 1968). Supplements to *The International Nietzsche Bibliography* were published in *Nietzsche-Studien. Internationales Jahrbuch für die Nietzsche-Forschung*, 2 (1973), 320–39, and 4 (1975), 351–73. Present plans call for a third,

So it was that the work progressed slowly, so slowly in fact, that the individual studies that I completed were written not as chapters of a book, but rather as autonomous articles for diverse journals. Nevertheless, I was not unduly concerned, for I felt that, with little additional effort, the differing formats could be brought into harmony. It was my belief that I had plenty of time. Unfortunately, I was wrong. Sudden terminal illness has numbered my days. Because of my personal crisis, the unfinished studies will now remain unfinished, and the finished essays will retain their original, disparate form.

My sadness at not being able to complete everything that I had set out to do has been considerably lessened by the fact that a growing number of scholars has in recent years been attracted to the general area of Nietzsche impact studies. In addition, it is consoling to know that the relationship of Morgenstern, Ernst, and Broch to Nietzsche has been examined in sound and comprehensive Masters' theses written under my direction.[2]

In all, there are five studies. Three of these deal with German authors, the dramatists Carl Sternheim and Georg Kaiser and the novelist Hermann Hesse; two deal with Austrians, the dramatist Arthur Schnitzler and the novelist Robert Musil. Fortunately, these five provide a fairly general coverage with regard to time, geographical location and genre.

Before concluding these remarks, I should like to make it very clear that what I have sought to do is not so much to show general similarity of viewpoint as to demonstrate real impact. Hence I have concentrated more on catch-words, slogans, themes, and motifs than on intriguing parallelisms in outlook or style that may or may not derive from Nietzsche. Let there be no mistake. I respect comparative studies and consider them important. However, I feel that Nietzsche was one of those unique individuals who not only mirror the *Zeitgeist*, but who through their unusually articulate, colorful and novel thoughts, help to form it. I believe that Nietzsche not only reflected the same cultural background as other eminent contemporaries, but, to a considerable extent, influenced his time, on an almost global

expanded edition of the *International Nietzsche Bibliography*, updated by David S. Thatcher of the University of Victoria, B.C., by the De Gruyter Publishing Company in Berlin in 1977.

[2] Irmen H. Horne, "Nietzsche und Christian Morgenstern" (M.A. Thesis, University of North Carolina, 1971), 115 pp. William F. Lowe, Jr., "The Ethic of Paul Ernst as Manifest in His Tragedies" (M.A. Thesis, University of North Carolina, 1965), 96 pp. George K. Miller, "Friedrich Nietzsche and Hermann Broch: Similarities and Influences" (M.A. Thesis, University of North Carolina, 1973), 76 pp.

scale. Thus, in the following studies I have discussed only such matters which, I feel, can reasonably be traced back to the inspiration of Nietzsche himself.

I would like to express my warm thanks to Dr. Barbara Eger and to Prof. Siegfried Mews for generous and expert editorial assistance.

Chapel Hill, North Carolina   January 1975

Nietzsche's *Geniemoral* and Schnitzler's Ethics [1]

In an article written in 1963, I sought in a very tentative fashion to demonstrate that Nietzsche had stimulated the thinking of the Austrian writer Arthur Schnitzler.[2] My introductory comments alluded to the fact that both approached *homo sapiens* from a strongly psychological viewpoint and that they shared such ideas as determinism, the subjective nature of truth, and the power of the subconscious. However, it was apparent to me that even if Schnitzler had derived all or a part of his psychological approach from Nietzsche, this could only be shown in a very circumstantial manner, as psychology and psychoanalysis were becoming generally popular, and Siegmund Freud lived only a few blocks away from Schnitzler in Vienna.[3]

I was particularly interested in ascertaining whether Nietzsche's unique *Geniemoral*, which had caught the fancy of so many writers of the time, had not also had some effect on Schnitzler. Reading through Schnitzler's work, it seemed at first that he himself was not going to be of much assistance. The references to Nietzsche were sparse and merely referred to him as an eminent modern thinker. The most detailed reference occurred in the novel *Der Weg ins Freie* (1903), in which friendly old Dr. Stauber mentioned favorably several ethical thinkers, including Nietzsche with his

[1] This study is essentially a reworking of an earlier article entitled "The Ethical Import of the Artist in the Works of Arthur Schnitzler," *Modern Austrian Literature*, 6/1-2 (1973), 123–50.

[2] "Nietzsche and Schnitzler," *Studies in Arthur Schnitzler*, University of North Carolina Studies in the Germanic Languages and Literatures, No. 42 (Chapel Hill: University of North Carolina Press, 1963), pp. 95–107.

[3] Gerd Klaus Schneider in his 1968 University of Washington dissertation, "Arthur Schnitzler und die Psychologie seiner Zeit unter besonderer Berücksichtigung der Philosophie Friedrich Nietzsches," deals with this similarity of psychological outlook. Schneider relies entirely on parallelism of thought to deduce Nietzschean impact. He is content to operate on the following hypothesis: "If it can be shown that Nietzsche's psychological insights are similar to the psychological theories as they existed in Schnitzler's time, then it is possible to assume that Nietzsche also influenced the psychologist Schnitzler" (cf. pp. 1 and 359).

Übermensch idea, but then added that he did not believe that any of these ideas were essentially new.[4] A careful survey of the plays, however, led me to believe that some impact by Nietzsche was possibly discernable in the *Geniemoral* of Schnitzler's artists and artist-types.

I developed this idea briefly in the article and, as was to be expected, the reaction of the critics to my thesis was mixed. I was disturbed to note, however, that William H. Rey in his comment stated that I had returned to the superficial and outmoded thinking of the hostile Schnitzler critics of the earlier part of the century.[5] Quite to the contrary, I felt that I was showing something new and, at the same time, favorable to Schnitzler. To remedy this misunderstanding I directed a second article[6] specifically at Rey's remarks, whereupon he was good enough to acknowledge the complexity of the situation in an understanding personal letter. Yet four years later a dissertation written under Rey's direction clearly rejected the notion that there could be a possible influence of Nietzsche's *Geniemoral* on Schnitzler's ethics.[7] To compound the confusion, other Schnitzler critics, in their desire to stress the ethical nature of Schnitzler's writing, were emphasizing the role the doctors and the doctor types as the author's principal spokesmen. Therefore, it seemed that the situation was getting blurred and that Schnitzler, rather than being wronged by me, was being done an injustice by his would-be benefactors. Schnitzler's "moral nature" was emphasized to such an extent that his quality and his depth as an artist were being overlooked. So for a third time I decided to investigate the ethical import of the artist in the works of Arthur Schnitzler.

In the following discussion, my comments will be directed towards answering three principal questions. First, does it seem likely or even possible that Nietzsche's *Geniemoral* influenced the morality of Schnitzler's artists and artist types? Second, is it conceivable that these artists are spokes-

[4] Arthur Schnitzler, *Die Erzählenden Schriften* (Frankfurt am Main: S. Fischer Verlag, 1961), I, 775. S. Fischer also published two volumes of *Die Dramatischen Werke* (1962) and one volume of *Aphorismen und Betrachtungen* (1967). Henceforth all page references to Schnitzler's published works will be to this edition and will appear in parentheses in the body of the text. The two volumes of dramatic works will be referred to as *DW* I and II, the two volumes of narrative prose as *ES* I and II, and the volume of aphorisms as *A*.

[5] William H. Rey, "Beiträge zur amerikanischen Schnitzlerforschung," *German Quarterly*, 37 (1964), 286–88.

[6] "Schnitzlers egoistische Künstlergestalten," *Journal of the International Arthur Schnitzler Research Association*, 4/2 (1965), 20–27.

[7] Cf. Schneider, pp. 31–37.

men for Schnitzler himself, or are they merely the object of his wrath? Third, to what extent do the doctors and doctor types serve as the author's mouthpiece?

One of Schnitzler's best known artists is Filippo Loschi in *Der Schleier der Beatrice* (1899), a poet of Bologna at the time of the Renaissance. He is presented as a genius whose poetry is highly esteemed by everyone in the city. At his death the Duke says of him:

> Ein Lied von dem, verweht's der Zufall nicht—
> Ist ew'ger als der kühnste unsrer Siege,
> Der wieder nur Vergängliches erringt!
>
> Denn dieser war ein Bote, ausgesandt,
> Das Grüßen einer hingeschwundnen Welt
> Lebendig jeder neuen zu bestellen
> Und hinzuwandeln über allen Tod. (*DW* I, 676–77)

Loschi himself is free of any doubts as to his ability. But his self-esteem as an artist seems to be the only thing about which his feelings do not waver, for he is a person of tempestuous passions and volatile emotions. He had worshipped his fiancée, the Countess Teresina Fantuzzi, and immortalized her in his verse. Then, in a pique he left her and at a street dance fell madly in love with a commoner, Beatrice Nardi. A few days later his ardor for Beatrice turned to ice when she naively revealed an unconscious admiration for the Duke. And so it continues.

However, Loschi's volatile and contradictory nature is neither petty nor insincere; he simply lives entirely in the experience of the moment. Thus, when he is filled with his love for Beatrice, he dreads the thought of death and purchases horses at an exorbitant price so that he and Beatrice can flee the besieged city. One might say that at this particular moment his love of life makes him a coward. Yet, not an hour later, when he becomes disillusioned with Beatrice, he gives the horses away, spends the night in revelry, and has no thought of leaving. Now he appears brash and heroic. Similarly, while in love with Beatrice he callously ignores all appeals to remember his vow to Teresina. But as soon as his love for Beatrice fades, he berates himself for having deserted Teresina, and seeks death at the hands of her brother.

Loschi's actions reflect not only his character but his outlook. He likens his moods to the changing seasons and views his vacillation as an expression of the law of nature:

Wer spricht von Schuld? Im Herbste fallen Blätter,
Im Frühjahr sprießen andre! Sagt Ihr drum,
Daß einer schuldig ward? Ich bin es nicht!
Es sei, daß Schuldigsein bedeutet: ew'gen
Gesetzen unterworfen sein. Ist's so,
Dann wartet Schuld von Kindheit auf in uns,
Wie unser Tod in unserm Busen harrt,
Solang wir atmen. Wenn ich schuldig bin,
So ist die Jugend ein Geschenk der Hölle,
Ist Schönheit Sünde und das Glück ein Gift,
So tückisch wie kein andres. (*DW* I, 561)

The only obligation he will acknowledge is to his own feelings of the moment:

Wahn ist nur eins: das nicht verlassen können,
Was uns nichts ist, ob Freund, ob Frau, ob Heimat,—
Und eins ist Wahrheit: Glück, woher es kommt! (*DW* I, 567)

He regards himself free of conventional restraints and above the common run of men: "Wo ich bin, gilt nicht, was unten/ Schicksal und Weg bestimmt" (*DW* I, 569). Rather than surrender Beatrice, he is prepared to sacrifice Bologna, "als meines Glückes würd'ger Opferbrand" (*ibid.*).

Whatever one feels about Loschi, the fact remains that morally considered he is a fickle egotist and a creature of whims. It must not be forgotten, however, that his bond with the fleeting moment also has a positive side, which may be seen in his profound awareness of the beauty and uniqueness of existence. Indeed, it would not be incorrect to say that his ethical vacillation was the necessary counterpart of his poetic insight.

Loschi's appreciation of life is most apparent in the scene in which Beatrice pleads with him that they die together. He knows what it is to lose life, to die. So terrible is this realization that he cannot believe Beatrice is aware of the full import of her words. Repeatedly he tries to impress upon her the meaning of her request and finally in desperation, convinced that she still does not understand, he resorts to a brutal ruse, pretending that the wine they have been drinking has been poisoned. Beatrice emits an anguished cry which he interprets as a sign of fright and panic. Completely disillusioned, he sends her back to the Duke and himself now really quaffs a poisoned draught. It is bitterly ironic that his final homage to life is to commit suicide. The Duke speaks in the spirit of Loschi when, going forth to do battle against hopeless odds, he says: "Das Leben ist die Fülle, nicht die Zeit,/ Und noch der nächste Augenblick ist weit!" (*DW* I, 679). These are the last lines of the play and express a basic theme.

Because of Loschi's importance to our understanding of Schnitzler's artists, we should like to quote one of the more significant passages which reveal the intensity and depth of his outlook:

> Nicht wunderlich, für dich nicht!—Nein!—Du bist
> Zu staunen nicht gemacht. Niemals hat dich
> Des Daseins Wunder namenlos erschreckt,
> Nie bist du vor der Buntheit dieser Welt
> In Andacht hingesunken, und daß du,
> Die Beatrice ist, und ich, Filippo,
> Sich unter den unendlich vielen fanden,
> Hat nie mit tiefem Schauer dich erfüllt. . . .
>
> All dies ist Dasein—das bist du, das ich,
> Hier unten ruht die Stadt, drin atmen Menschen,
> Dort stürzt ins Weite Straß' und Straße hin
> Ins Land, ans Meer,—und überm Wasser wieder
> Menschen und Städte;—ober uns gebreitet
> Dies blauende Gewölbe und sein Glanz,
> Und alles dies ist unser, denn wir sind!
> Und morgen schon gehört es uns so wenig,
> Als alles Lichtes Wunderfülle Blinden,
> Gelähmten aller Wege Lust und Fernen. (*DW* I, 634–35)

Thus we are presented with the strange dilemma that it is the fickle and egotistical artist alone who can fully appreciate the miracle of life and the incomprehensible annihilation of death.

Not long thereafter Schnitzler portrayed the Renaissance artist anew in the one-act play, *Die Frau mit dem Dolche* (1900). This artist, an unknown master who died around 1530, comes briefly to life in the day-dream of a young woman.

Pauline, the wife of an acclaimed playwright, has met her admirer Leonhard in an art gallery. Leonhard seeks to win her by making it clear that her husband is a consummate egotist who has twice betrayed her. Not only did he deceive her with another woman, but then when Pauline forgave him, he used the episode as the basis of his successful play, exposing her to public ridicule. Yet Pauline is proud of her husband and sure of his love.

But as she gazes up at a beautiful painting above her bearing the caption, "Die Frau mit dem Dolche," she suddenly identifies with the character and relives the scene. It is she, Paola, who has stabbed the young man, her lover, out of a sense of shame and frustration. Why? Because her returning husband had not taken offense and avenged her when Lionhardo not only confessed that he had slept with her but insisted that her painter-husband Remigio exact the full penalty. To her consternation, Remigio's sole reaction to the confession had been "Gleichgültigkeit" (DW I, 716) and to the stabbing, ecstatic joy over her graceful pose which is just what he needed for his painting:

> War dies der Sinn? Ist mein Gebet erhört,
> Daß für mein Bildnis mir Erleuchtung werde?
> Ja, so vollend' ich's! Der du dies gefügt,
> O Himmel, eine Stunde lang gewähre
> Der Seele Frieden, Ruhe dieser Hand. (DW I, 718)

Recovering from her day-dream, Pauline considers for a moment and then without love but with a sense of determination, promises Leonhard the tryst he has sought. She now realizes that all artists, including her husband, are inherent egotists true only to their art.

The theme of the nature of the artist is taken up in another one-act play written in the same year, *Lebendige Stunden*. Rather than being a Renaissance virtuoso, the protagonist Heinrich is a young contemporary writer who has not yet made a name for himself. It is clear, however, that he is to be considered as a representative of the true artist; this is evident from the statements of his opponent Hausdorfer who is angry with him but admits his uniqueness. After rhetorically asking the gardener Borromäus whether he knew what it meant to be a poet, Hausdorfer says: "Nichts wissen Sie, gar nichts. Wir wissen das alle nicht, wir gewöhnlichen Menschen, die nichts weiter können als ihre Gärten bepflanzen . . ." (DW I, 692). Although it has been an easy matter to replace him, Hausdorfer, just another white-collar worker when he had retired, it was not always so easy to replace a poet who is a rare and unique being:

Aber ein Dichter—das ist schon eine andere Art von Mensch wie unsereiner, Borromäus. Wenn so einer in Pension geht, kann's passieren, daß die Stelle recht lang unbesetzt bleibt. Ja, so einer muß auf sich schauen, das ist er der Welt schuldig—verstehen S', Borromäus? (DW I, 693)

9

It is because Hausdorfer considers Heinrich to be a real artist that he doubts the latter's protestations of sorrow over his mother's death. "Ich kenne dich! Euch alle kenn' ich, ich weiß, wie ihr seid" (*DW* I, 697), Hausdorfer asserts and explains what he means, by relating how a composer he knew had written a song while his only child lay dead in the same room. Such behavior has convinced Hausdorfer that all artists are arrogant egotists: "Seid ihr nicht einer wie der andere? Hochmütig seid ihr—das ist es: hochmütig, alle, die Großen wie die Kleinen!" (*DW* I, 702). The events of the play justify Hausdorfer's belief, for it develops that Heinrich has virtually murdered his invalid mother. By failing to conceal his sense of frustration at having to care for her when he could have been writing, he induces her to take an overdose of morphium.

But again the artist has a more favorable side. With respect to the composer, it is not sure that Schnitzler agreed with Hausdorfer's interpretation of the apparently callous composer's feelings. Certainly, the words of the composer when he entered, "Hören Sie, Herr Hausdorfer, das ist für mein armes Buberl. Grad ist mir die Melodie eingefallen" (*DW* I, 698), do not necessarily indicate that he was devoid of feeling. As Schnitzler once said in defining the artist, "Beim *Dichter* ist die *Linie des Lebens* und des *Schaffens ein und dieselbe*" (*A*, 150).

Even more significant for an understanding of the artist as presented in the play is the final confrontation between Hausdorfer and Heinrich. The former contends that a few hours of the sick mother's life were worth more than all of Heinrich's art. Heinrich replies with dignity and passion:

> Lebendige Stunden? Sie leben doch nicht länger als der letzte, der sich ihrer erinnert. Es ist nicht der schlechteste Beruf, solchen Stunden Dauer zu verleihen, über ihre Zeit hinaus.—Leben Sie wohl, Herr Hausdorfer. Ihr Schmerz gibt Ihnen heute noch das Recht, mich mißzuverstehen. Im Frühjahr, wenn Ihr Garten aufs neue blüht, sprechen wir uns wieder. Denn auch Sie leben weiter. (*DW* I, 702)

Heinrich is convinced that it is the noble task of the artist to preserve the fleeting beauty of such "living hours," and that when Hausdorfer has gotten over his sorrow, he will recognize this fact. As in the case of Loschi, the egotism of the artist is grounded in his existential awareness and his dedication to art.

Perhaps Schnitzler's most penetrating analysis of the artist is to be found in *Der einsame Weg* (1904). There are several artist-figures in this play, but the one most fully characterized is the painter Julian Fichtner who has the spark of genius. This is attested to by the wise and gentle artist and art-critic, Professor Wegrat. In the latter's opinion, Fichtner was the "most promising" artist he had ever known. To Dr. Reumann's assertion that people usually manage to achieve what they are capable of achieving, Wegrat had this answer:

> Nicht immer. Julian war gewiß zu Höherem bestimmt. Was ihm gefehlt hat, war die Fähigkeit, sich zu sammeln, der innere Friede. Er konnte sich nirgends dauernd heimisch fühlen; und das Unglück war, daß er sich auch in seinen Arbeiten sozusagen nur vorübergehend aufhielt. (*DW* I, 772)

In personality and attitude Fichtner resembles his forebears, Loschi, Remigio and Heinrich. He had been passionately in love with his friend Wegrat's fiancée, Gabriele, and then, suddenly awakening as if from a state of intoxication, deserted her the night before their intended elopement. He terminated a second love-affair abruptly when he learned that his sweetheart, the actress Irene Herms, had while on tour shown a passing interest in another man. Like his fellows, Fichtner is an egocentric, fickle, ruthless artist. He has had only one purpose, one love in life: his art. He admitted jilting Gabriele because he feared that marriage would interfere with his career. Without a hint of pathos or remorse, he stated that had she committed suicide on his account, the sacrifice would not have been too great. Indeed, he says the days after his desertion were among the happiest and most rewarding in his life (*DW* I, 811–12).

In the play Fichtner is past his prime; his artistic powers have waned, his goals have faded. The inner fire no longer suffices and he has become lonely. He now seeks the affection of his son who has lived all these years as the child of another. His attempt meets with failure. Felix chooses to remain with his kindly foster-father, Professor Wegrat, who has shown him so much love and affection.

Is Fichtner castigated more harshly than his predecessors? Has Schnitzler changed his attitude toward the artist? We think not. Let us examine the facts.

There is nothing either petty or dissembling about Fichtner. Particularly in his heart-to-heart talk with his son Felix, in which he tells the latter the entire story of his desertion of Gabriele, he is honest and sincere. Although he hopes to win Felix as his friend, his words remain calm, devoid of sentimentality or false pathos. He does not seek to justify or minimize his guilt—it is here that he says that the sacrifice of Gabriele's life would not have been too great for the end involved. It is here that he admits having felt no remorse for his deed.

But how can we truly tell what is in the heart of a man when he is his own witness? We cannot. And so it is important to consult the opinion of another character, the artist von Sala, often viewed as the best self-portrait of Schnitzler himself. Von Sala is a sophisticated, rather reserved dramatist who eschews sentimentality and hypocrisy. His career has been marked with success, but his wife and daughter have died and he, too, is now aging and lonely. It must be observed that in all matters of social intercourse and etiquette von Sala has observed the proper forms, and he has the admiration and respect of his friends.

Von Sala has known Fichtner for many years, has in fact been closer to him than almost any other person, although his reserve prevents him from thinking in terms of such sentimental relationships as friendship:

> Sie wissen ja, daß Sie mir viel lieber sind als die meisten andern Menschen. Wir bringen einander die Stichworte so geschickt—finden Sie nicht? Es gibt pathetische Leute, die solche Beziehungen Freundschaft nennen. Übrigens ist es nicht unmöglich, daß wir uns im vorigen Jahrhundert "du" gesagt, am Ende gar, daß Sie sich an meinem Busen ausgeweint hätten. (*DW* I, 780)

Formerly, when Fichtner had not been on one of his frequent journeys, the two men had taken long walks together and discussed "die tiefst' und höchsten Dinge dieser Welt" (*ibid.*). Thus it is apparent that von Sala is a brusquely honest and unsentimental person who is intimately familiar with Fichtner. What is his judgment?

He tells Fichtner that he has no right to his son's affection, but that his only guilt lies in the fact that he is an artist, that he is a person who despite the best of intentions cannot be unselfish, cannot give of himself, cannot truly love, and must inevitably face old age alone. These words are no mere attempt at consolation, for von Sala is speaking not only to Fichtner, he is also speaking to himself. At bottom he feels, Fichtner and he are two of a kind who have belonged to no one and who are damned in old age to loneliness. Even if Felix had consented to view Fichtner as his father, even if the latter had a wife by his side, and children and grandchildren at his feet, indeed even if he were surrounded by bacchantes, he would still have to face old age alone:

Und was hülfe es Ihnen, wenn er [*Felix*] bliebe? Was hülfe es Ihnen selbst, wenn er irgend etwas wie kindliche Zärtlichkeit zu Ihnen empfände? . . . Und wenn Sie eine Frau an Ihrer Seite hätten, wären Sie heute nicht allein? . . . Und wenn Kinder und Enkel um Sie lebten, wären Sie es nicht? . . . Und wenn Sie sich Ihren Reichtum, Ihren Ruhm, Ihr Genie bewahrt hätten—wären Sie es nicht? . . . Und wenn uns ein Zug von Bacchanten begleitet—*den Weg hinab gehen wir alle allein . . . wir, die selbst niemandem gehört haben.* (*DW* I, 826; emphasis added)

For the egotistical artist is incapable of experiencing love:

Was hat das, was unsereiner in die Welt bringt, mit Liebe zu tun? Es mag allerlei Lustiges, Verlogenes, Zärtliches, Gemeines, Leidenschaftliches sein, das sich als Liebe ausgibt—aber Liebe ist es doch nicht . . . Haben wir jemals ein Opfer gebracht, von dem nicht unsere Sinnlichkeit oder unsere Eitelkeit ihren Vorteil gehabt hätte? . . . Haben wir je gezögert, anständige Menschen zu betrügen oder zu belügen, wenn wir dadurch um eine Stunde des Glücks oder der Lust reicher werden konnten? . . . Mein lieber Julian, wir haben die Türen offen stehen und unsere Schätze sehen lassen—aber Verschwender sind wir nicht gewesen. Sie so wenig als ich. Wir können uns ruhig die Hände reichen, Julian. (*DW* I, 826–27)

It may be argued that even von Sala lacks the proper perspective to judge Fichtner objectively. In this case, we may turn once again to Professor Wegrat, the director of the art academy, who combines in his personality the "Beamten" and the artist—as he says ironically of himself: "Der malt jedes Jahr sein braves Bild für die Ausstellung und kann beim besten Willen nicht anders" (*DW* I, 772). Wegrat is both insider and outsider. He is an artist of sorts but he is also a deeply unselfish person—like Doctor Reumann. And so when Reumann pointedly remarks, referring to Fichtner, that it was a moot question who fostered art and aided the world more, "Beamte wie Sie, Herr Professor, oder . . . die sogenannten Genies" (*DW* I, 772), Wegrat's reply is of utmost importance. Eschewing false modesty, he insists that the accomplishments of the genius stand above discussion—like the elements: "O, es fällt mir gar nicht ein, den Bescheidenen zu spielen. Aber was die Genies anbelangt, von denen wollen wir lieber nicht reden. Das ist eine Welt für sich und außerhalb der Diskussion—wie die Elemente" (*DW* I, 772).

In Wegrat's opinion, Fichtner was an artistic genius. If he had achieved only moderate success in his life-time, that was to be attributed to his innate restlessness. If he appeared irresponsible and egotistical, that was not for the likes of Reumann or himself to judge. The genius stands outside the bounds of convention.

While writing *Der einsame Weg*, Schnitzler was also at work on his novel, *Der Weg ins Freie* (1908), a good part of which was completed in 1903. Hence it is not altogether surprising to discover in the novel a pair of artists, Georg von Wergenthin and Hermann Bermann who, although considerably younger than Fichtner and von Sala, have a relationship somewhat similar to that which exists between the latter two. Wergenthin, twenty-seven years old, is a composer, musician and conductor whose songs have already won some critical acclaim. He possesses talent and deeply loves music. As the novel ends he is happily advancing to his first major position as conductor of the orchestra at the court theater in Detmold.

Wergenthin is superficially considerate and tender, but he cannot really give of himself. In his affair with Anna Rosner—a main theme in the novel—he resembles Fichtner. From the beginning he knows it will be a passing affair like the others: "Denn daß auch dieses Abenteur, so ernst und hold es begonnen, zu einem Ende bestimmt war, wußte Georg selbst in dieser Stunde, nur ohne jeden Schauer" (*ES* I, 712). As with his former sweethearts, he experiences a sense of freedom when he leaves Anna:

> Ein ähnliches Gefühl der Befreitheit kam freilich beinahe jedesmal über ihn, wenn er, auch nach schönerem Zusammensein, von einer Geliebten Abschied nahm. Selbst als er Anna an ihrem Haustor verlassen hatte, vor drei Tagen, nach dem ersten Abend vollkommenen Glücks, war er sich, früher als jeder anderen Regung, der Freude bewußt geworden, wieder allein zu sein. Und gleich darauf, ehe noch das Gefühl des Danks und die Ahnung einer wirklichen Zusammengehörigkeit mit diesem sanften, sein ganzes Wesen mit so viel Innigkeit umschließenden Geschöpf in seiner Seele emporzudringen vermochte, flog durch sie ein sehnsuchtsvoller Traum von Fahrten über ein schimmerndes Meer, von Küsten, die sich verführerisch nähern, von Spaziergängen an Ufern, . . . von blauen Fernen, *Ungebundenheit und Alleinsein*. (*ES* I, 712; emphasis added)

During Anna's pregnancy, Georg has moments when he is convinced that he is deeply in love with her (*ES* I, 823), but he is generally more inclined to view the whole situation as a "Malheur." At times he simply puts her out of his mind and on one occasion composes a song "als Anna und das Kind für ihn völlig vergessen waren" (*ES* I, 951). On a warm summer night he is attracted to Therese Golowski and, almost in Anna's sight, kisses Therese in frustrated desire: "Ihre Lippen ruhten aufeinander, einen kurzen

Augenblick, der mehr erfüllt war von der wehen Lust der Lüge als von irgend einer andern" (*ES* I, 822). Not long thereafter, the mention of another old flame sets Georg's heart to pounding: "Der Name Sissy zuckte an Georgs Herzen vorbei, wie ein glitzernder Dolch. Er wußte es plötzlich, in wenig Tagen würde er bei ihr sein. Seine Sehnsucht schwoll so mächtig auf, daß er es selbst kaum begriff" (*ES* I, 844). When the child arrives it is still-born, and Anna experiences great mental anguish and physical suffering. Nevertheless, only a short time later Georg returns her to her parents and with no feeling of remorse sets out on his new career:

> Georg aber war es gut und frei zumut. Er faßte den Entschluß, die drei Tage, die jetzt ihm gehörten, so vernünftig als möglich auszunützen. Das beste war wohl, irgendwo in einer schönen, stillen Landschaft allein zu sein, auszuruhen und sich zur neuen Arbeit zu sammeln . . . In Georgs Seele war ein mildes Abschiednehmen von mancherlei Glück und Leid . . . und zugleich ein Grüßen unbekannter Tage, die aus der Weite der Welt seiner Jugend entgegenklangen. (*ES* I, 958)

In the same lightly ironic way that von Sala understands Fichtner, Bermann understands Wergenthin and absolves him of guilt:

> Und ich versichre Sie . . . Sie haben damit gewiß keine sogenannte Schuld auf sich geladen. Bei einem andern wär es vielleicht Schuld gewesen. Aber bei Ihnen, der von Natur aus—Sie verzeihen schon—ziemlich leichtfertig und ein bißchen gewissenlos angelegt ist, war es gewiß nicht Schuld. (*ES* I, 957)

Whereas Fichtner and Wergenthin have much in common, they are not like two peas in a pod. The former was characterized as a genius too restless to realize his full potential, the latter is ultimately seen to be more interested in appreciating and understanding music than in composing. Wergenthin reaches this understanding of himself while attending a performance of *Tristan and Isolde*:

> Wußte er denn, ob ihm gegeben war Menschen durch seine Kunst zu zwingen, wie dem Meister, der sich heute hier vernehmen ließ? Sieger zu werden über das Bedenkliche, Klägliche, Jammervolle des Alltags? Ungeduld und Zweifel wollten aus seinem Innern emporsteigen; doch rasch bannten Wille und Einsicht sie von dannen, und nun fühlte er sich wieder so rein beglückt wie immer, wenn er schöne Musik hörte, ohne daran zu

denken, daß er selbst oft als Schöpfer wirken und gelten wollte. Von allen seinen Beziehungen zu der geliebten Kunst blieb in solchen Ausgenblicken nur die eine übrig, *sie mit tieferem Verstehen aufnehmen zu dürfen, als irgend ein anderer Mensch.* Und er fühlte, daß Heinrich die Wahrheit gesprochen hatte, als sie zusammen durch einen von Morgentau feuchten Wald gefahren waren: *nicht schöpferische Arbeit,—die Atmosphäre seiner Kunst allein war es, die ihm zum Dasein nötig war;* kein Verdammter war er wie Heinrich, den es immer trieb zu fassen, zu formen, zu bewahren, und dem die Welt in Stücke zerfiel, wenn sie seiner gestaltenden Hand entgleiten wollte. (*ES* I, 921; emphasis added)

To repeat: Wergenthin comes to the realization that his ultimate objective is the understanding and appreciation of music. Does this imply that he is a pseudo-artist, comparable to the *Literat* in the field of creative writing? We do not think so. Wergenthin has, in analyzing himself, virtually given a definition of the born conductor. His strength lies not in creation but in interpretation. What is of greatest importance: *his heart is in his art*, his music, whether in creating or in interpreting, and not with such matters as power, wealth, advancement or intrigue. Wergenthin is in the last analysis an artist,[8] even if perhaps not the greatest. But in delineating the nature of the artist, it will be recalled that Hausdorfer made no neat distinctions. For him artists were essentially alike, great and small. To confirm this line of reasoning, we have the same recourse as in *Der einsame Weg* to consider the greater artist, in this case Heinrich Bermann.[9]

[8] Even if one were to conclude that Wergenthin is an aesthete and dilettante rather than an artist, he is no more selfish or narcissistic than the true artists, so that the ethical import remains the same.

[9] As in the case of von Sala, Bermann is frequently identified with Schnitzler. Cf. for example the essay by H. B. Garland, "Arthur Schnitzler," *German Men of Letters*, II, ed. Alex Natan (London, 1963), p. 72: "Heinrich Bermann, the Jewish author, has long been known as a self-portrait, and the tormenting relationship with the actress, the sadistic refusal alike to forgive or to relinquish, and the conclusion in her suicide are closely paralleled by an episode in Schnitzler's life." Garland believes that the author projected "facets of his own erotic life into two sharply differentiated characters" and that not only Bermann's but also von Wergenthin's "erotic life is unmistakably that of his creator." Françoise Derré, *L'Oeuvre d'Arthur Schnitzler* (Paris, 1966) notes that Bermann is "l'un des plus étroitement liés aussi á Georg von Wergenthin" (p. 260). Although she feels that Bermann's discussion of the need to avoid truth in drama reflects Schnitzler's view on the subject and is a "défense anticipée et ironique de *Professor Bernhardi*" (p. 263), she is careful not to make him one with his author. The fact is that Schnitzler outwardly sought to distance himself from Bermann, describing the latter as follows: "ein hagerer, bartloser Mensch mit düsteren Augen und mit etwas zu langem schlichtem Haar . . . und dessen Gebaren und

We have already seen that Wergenthin viewed the thirty-year old playwright "auf dem Wege zum Ruhm" (*ES* I, 942) as a "Verdammter ... den es immer trieb zu fassen, zu formen, zu bewahren" (*ES* I, 921). Bermann himself makes it clear that the only moments he, with his cynical and pessimistic cast of mind, really treasures are those of creative activity. Although he is quite ready to admit that "Ruhm, Reichtum, Wirkung in die Weite" are things that are illusory and can be dispensed with, he is unwilling to give up his faith in "etwas so Unzweifelhaftes ... wie es die Augenblicke des innern Kraftgefühls sind" (*ES* I, 694). When the older and highly successful novelist Nürnberger seeks to elicit a disavowal with the remark: "Inneres Kraftgefühl! Warum sagen Sie nicht gleich Seligkeit des Schaffens?" Bermann calmly retorts: "Gibts, Nürnberger!"

Like Loschi, the playwright is brusquely honest and of vascillating mood. At times he despises himself. "Und wenn das einmal geschehen ist, gibt es keinen Tropf und keinen Schurken, mit dem wir uns nicht innerlich gegen uns selbst verbünden" (*ES* I, 670–71). At other times he feels superior and immune to conventional assessment: "Es gibt auch andre Stimmungen, in denen mir überhaupt nichts und niemand etwas anhaben kann. Da hab ich nur dieses eine Gefühl: was wißt Ihr denn alle, was wißt Ihr denn von mir ..." (*ES* I, 671).

Like von Sala with Fichtner, Bermann considers himself essentially similar in character to Wergenthin. It is significant that in the quotation given above, in which he berates himself, he had continued: "Entschuldigen Sie, wenn ich 'wir' sage ...." Bermann's character is particularly well illuminated in his relations with his distant actress-sweetheart. He writes her long and recriminatory letters accusing her of being unfaithful, but he has no desire to marry her or even to be with her, as he prefers "lieber Schmerzen als Verantwortungen" (*ES* I, 729). Although because of her he experiences "Qualen der Eifersucht," he has no compunctions at spending his evenings with an attractive blonde—"um sich zu betäuben" (*ES* I, 708). A passage in a letter from the actress that hints at infidelity causes him more anguish than his deranged father who is confined to a mental institution or his mother and sister "die verzweifeln" (*ES* I, 679); but when the actress visits him to effect a reconciliation, he coldly rejects her. Her threats of

Aussehen ... an einen fanatischen jüdischen Lehrer aus der Provinz erinnerte" (*ES* I, 647), unelegant in dress and tactless in his behaviour. Nevertheless Bermann shares with Schnitzler his keen knowledge of the human psyche, his pessimism and scepticism, and his dedication to art.

suicide leave him unmoved, and when she ultimately takes her life, he stoutly denies any guilt:

> Denken Sie, eine Frau, die Sie liebt, würde Sie verfolgen, eine Frau, vor deren Berührung Ihnen aus irgendeinem Grunde graut, würde Ihnen schwören, sie bringt sich um, wenn Sie sie verschmähen. Wären Sie verpflichtet ihr nachzugeben? Könnten Sie sich den leisesten Vorwurf machen, wenn sie wirklich aus sogenannter verschmähter Liebe in den Tod ginge? Würden Sie sich als ihr Mörder fühlen? Das ist doch lauter Unsinn, nicht wahr? Also wenn Sie glauben, daß es das sogennannte Gewissen ist, das mich jetzt peinigt, so irren Sie sich. (*ES* I, 893)

After the suicide Heinrich is in strangely good humor, which Nürnberger attributes to the fact that tragic events may indirectly flatter the vanity of "such individuals," who may even feel that the event can be of value to their art:

> Menschen, die sich so viel, fast ausschließlich mit sich selbst beschäftigen wie er, verwinden ja seelische Schmerzen überraschend schnell. Auf solchen Naturen, und wohl nicht nur auf solchen, lastet das geringfügigste physische Unbehagen viel drückender als jede Art von Herzenspein, selbst Untreue und Tod geliebter Personen. Es rührt wohl daher, daß jeder Seelenschmerz irgendwie unserer Eitelkeit schmeichelt, was man von einem Typhus oder einem Magenkatarrh nicht behaupten kann. Und beim Künstler kommt vielleicht dazu, daß aus einem Magenkatarrh absolut nichts zu holen ist . . . (*ES* I, 931)

It is clear from the passage that Nürnberger views Heinrich as a typical egocentric artist.[10]

Bermann was also egotistical in his relations with other people, as Wergenthin realized earlier, accustomed to associating with them only as long as they provided a suitable subject "für seine psychologischen Interessen" and then dropping them again "mit der größten Rücksichtslosigkeit" when he felt like it (*ES* I, 768).

It should be clear, then, that Wergenthin and Bermann, like Fichtner and von Sala, differ in their personality and in their ability, but they do have one basic thing in common: they both are changeable, ruthless, egotistical

---

[10] Nürnberger is at first referring to the egotist *per se*, but his final sentence makes it clear what he says is particularly true of the artist—and that Nürnberger has the artist particularly in mind.

artists. They are also counterparts to von Sala and Fichtner in their capacity as aging artists, who must pay the price for their egotism in unloved loneliness.

Georg Merklin in *Der Puppenspieler* (1906) is also such a person. In his prime he toyed with the affections of those who loved him, arrogantly fancying that he was playing the role of destiny in their lives. Years later, he discovers that destiny has played a joke on him: the less gifted but also less selfish objects of his fun-making have gained the warmth and affection of family life, while he is doomed to loneliness. However, as one can argue that there is no evidence that he is really talented or that his contempt for the hack-writing he does is not just another case of "sour grapes," we will turn to an aging artist of real stature, Casanova.

As William Rey has pointed out,[11] the great lover in the novella, *Casanovas Heimfahrt* (1918), is not only a genius in the erotic sphere, he has the potential to be a genius in many areas:

> Ja, hätte er in jüngeren Jahren Muße und Geduld gehabt, sich mit derlei Arbeiten ernstlicher zu beschäftigen,—das wußte er wohl—den ersten dieses Fachs, Dichtern und Philosophen, hätte er es gleichgetan: ebenso wie er als Finanzmann oder Diplomat mit größerer Beharrlichkeit und Vorsicht, als ihm eigen war, zum Höchsten wäre berufen gewesen. (*ES* II, 269)

Casanova resembles Fichtner in his lack of patience. But whereas the latter grew restless for a change of scene, Casanova threw "alle seine Lebenspläne hin, wenn ein neues Liebesabenteuer lockte" (*ES* II, 269).

In the novella, Casanova has grown old, his skin has become yellow and wrinkled, the girls no longer smile at him, and his pride has suffered. But in his tremendous egotism, his almost heroic arrogance, he refuses to yield. The story deals with one incident in his futile battle against old age and death.

The beautiful and intelligent Marcolina has displayed disinterest and even a trace of disgust in his presence. Enraged, Casanova devises an ingenious and successful scheme to win her for a night. In the dark Marcolina believes that she is with her young lover, the lieutenant Lorenzi. But Casanova's vanity induces him to remain with Marcolina, rather than to leave as originally planned before dawn. He falls asleep and when he awakens the girl is looking down at him in shame and disgust. Had her eyes

---

[11] William H. Rey, *Arthur Schnitzler* (Berlin, 1968), p. 32.

said "Dieb-Wüstling-Schurke" his ego would have survived, but her glance reveals only the two words "Alter Mann" (ES II, 310). Humiliated he takes his leave, to be stopped a few moments later by Lorenzi who challenges him to a duel. Casanova senses danger but has no fear. Seeing the handsome youth standing there, the image of himself thirty years earlier, to whom only hours before he had said "Wir sind vom gleichen Stoff gemacht, sind Brüder im Geiste" (ES II, 296), Casanova is tempted to throw away his sword and embrace Lorenzi. But the latter's eyes are cold and the duel begins. The lieutenant appears like a young God and Casanova's sense of frustration reawakens. With the thought, "Er ist nur jung, ich aber bin Casanova" he stabs Lorenzi through the heart (ES II, 313). He looks down at the dead youth for a moment, murmurs "Glücklicher," and then kisses him on the forehead (ES II, 314). The futility of his action has become apparent to him; for the egocentric artist there is no escape from the despair and loneliness of old age.

As Lorenzi is the mirror image of Casanova when he was young, it is understandable that he shares the latter's egotistical and, one is tempted to stress, Nietzschean *Geniemoral*. Casanova had quickly recognized this similarity of outlook:

> Sie haben gar keine Vorurteile, so wenig als ich sie habe oder jemals hatte; und was ich von Ihnen zu verlangen willens bin, ist nichts andres, als was ich selbst an Ihrer Stelle unter den gleichen Umständen zu erfüllen mich keinen Augenblick besonnen hätte,—wie ich mich auch tatsächlich nie gescheut habe, wenn es das Schicksal oder auch nur meine Laune so forderte, eine Schurkerei zu begehen oder vielmehr das, was die Narren dieser Erde so zu nennen pflegen. (*ES* II, 296)

Lorenzi demonstrates his "immoralism" by making love on the same night to Marcolina, whom he adores, and to the Marchesa, from whom he accepts expensive gifts. He betrays Marcolina to Casanova in order to free himself from embarrassment and debt, and then later gives his life in a duel to save her honor. Like Filippo Loschi, Casanova and Lorenzi lend their actions dignity, despite their total disregard for conventional standards, by their willingness to stake their lives on the outcome (*ES* II, 296).

A striking parallel to Casanova may be seen in the protagonist of a play written eight years earlier, *Das weite Land*. Hofreiter, a factory owner, is anything but the typical captain of industry. The detailed stage directions make it evident that he is an artist type:

Schlank, nicht sehr groß, schmales, feines Gesicht, dunkler Schnurrbart, englisch gestutzt; blondes grau meliertes, rechts gescheiteltes Haar. Er trägt Zwicker ohne Band, den er manchmal abnimmt; geht etwas nach vorn gebeugt. Kleine, ein wenig zusammengekniffene Augen. Liebenswürdige weiche, beinahe weichliche Art zu reden, die manchmal ins ironisch Bissige umschlägt. Seine Bewegungen sind geschmeidig, aber verraten Energie. Er ist mit Eleganz, ganz ohne Geckenhaftigkeit gekleidet. (*DW* II, 228)

His friend, Dr. Mauer attests to his great charm: "Ich mag mich über ihn noch so rasend geärgert haben,—sobald er seine Charmeurkünste spielen läßt, bin ich ihm doch wieder ausgeliefert auf Gnade und Ungnade" (*DW* II, 248).

Like Casanova, Hofreiter experiences the thrill of life in erotic adventures and, again like Casanova, undergoes with advancing age the frustrations of the egotist. Although in his case the girl, Erna, is willing, Hofreiter realizes—as Casanova did not—that to have an affair would not bridge the gap of age, would not give him back his youth. And so he renounces. But his frustration is as bitter as Casanova's and vents itself in the same way. For no other reason than his hatred of triumphant youth, he kills the young lover of his wife.

Lastly, let us consider the writer Anastasius Treuenhof, in Schnitzler's posthumously published drama, *Das Wort*, on which the author began to work around 1901 and continued at intervals to work until shortly before his death in 1931.[12] Schnitzler's notes of 1920 reveal that he conceived of Treuenhof (modelled after Peter Altenberg) as a true artist: "Treuenhof soll ja der einzige sein, der Talent hat, die anderen haben nur Willen."[13] Kurt Bergel reasons that Schnitzler never published the play because he could not reconcile the portrait of the artist with an incident that required the superficiality and irresponsibility of the *Literat*:

Einmal wollte er das Porträt eines Dichters geben mit all dem Genialen und auch Scharlatanhaften, all dem Feingefühl und der Selbstsucht, die dem Original im Café Central eigen waren. Andererseits hatte er einen 'Vorfall,' der die Oberflächlichkeit und Verantwortungslosigkeit des Literaten bloßlegte. Um die Unverantwortlichkeit, die im Mißbrauch des Wortes liegt, überzeugend darzustellen, mußte Schnitzler seinem Treuenhof einen

---

[12] *Das Wort*, ed. Kurt Bergel (Frankfurt am Main, 1966), p. 5.
[13] *Ibid.*, p. 15.

großen Teil seiner Sympathie entziehen: so wurde dieser immer mehr zum Literaten, so daß man ihm schließlich weder Genie noch menschliche Wärme zu glauben vermag.[14]

Excluding, then, the last scene in which Treuenhof causes Willi to commit suicide, we see again a brilliant, egotistical, ruthlessly honest artist who cannot with the best of intentions give of himself, who esteems the beauty of life in all its dismal meaninglessness, and who ends alone.

To recapitulate: we have presented a sampling of the more important artist types in Schnitzler's writings. They are all different, each possessed of his own individuality. At the same time, they all have certain things in common: disdain for the common man, disregard for all men, and an overwhelming self-esteem. Fickle and passionate, they have a deep appreciation for the beauty of life and the experience of the moment. They live only for their art, whether this be painting, writing, or love-making— in a sense, they are true disciples of Nietzsche and his *Geniemoral*.

The question now arises: to what extent, if any, does the artist-figure represent a projection of Schnitzler's basic views? How relevant is the portrayal of the artist to the author's ethical outlook? One must proceed with caution, as it obviously does not follow that a character necessarily expresses or represents an author's views. Specific evidence must be supplied to indicate the contrary, if we are not to assume that an author has created freely from his imagination. We believe, however, that in the present instance such evidence is available. Here is our reasoning.

To begin with, the freedom of the writer is a strange thing. It is actually rare that one encounters a serious writer who does not deal with issues that lie close to his heart. Even the so-called notable exceptions, like Zola and Georg Kaiser, when examined closely, do not violate this rule; the idea, for example, that Zola proceeded with scientific objectivity in writing *Les Rougon-Macquart* or that Georg Kaiser was truly a *Denkspieler* has largely been discounted.

Furthermore, some authors are less free in dealing with their subject matter than others. In fact, a number get so involved with their creations that the characters seem to take on a life of their own. It appears that Schnitzler was a subjective writer of this sort. Certainly, it is interesting to note that although Otto Brahm several times requested he write a comedy,

---

[14] *Ibid.*, p. 26. Indeed, Schnitzler felt that Altenberg was a unique combination of *Dichter* and *Literat*.

and, that it would have been decidedly to Schnitzler's advantage to do so, his plays invariably ended up as tragi-comedies.

Such general arguments as these do not, of course, prove anything. But they do suggest the possibility that Schnitzler may have been seriously interested in his artist-figures and may even, to a degree, have identified with them.

If Schnitzler had disavowed his artists on moral grounds, as has sometimes been maintained, it would seem to imply that he attributed to his artist-figures a degree of moral free will. Yet this rarely seems to be the case. Indeed, few of his characters have any large measure of free will; they live in a world of dreams and illusions and are frequently controlled by their emotions. Even his most voluntaristic protagonists appear as puppets in the hands of destiny. Helene, in *Der junge Medardus* (1910), for example, professes to believe only in the strong assertion of the will: "Es gibt kein Glück, es gibt nur den Willen, das Schicksal zu zwingen. Es gibt keine Freunde;—nur den Willen, über Menschen Herr zu sein. Der Wille ist alles, Bertrand" (*DW* II, 136). Yet she yields despite herself to the impulse of love and her courageous plans are thwarted by tragic misunderstanding. Her lover, Medardus, is also a defiant voluntarist, but he, too, falls victim to his feelings and tragic coincidence, so that ultimately his freedom is restricted to dying a meaningless death in defiance of Napoleon.

To be sure, if we turn to some of the later utterances, such as the section *Schicksal und Wille* in *Buch der Sprüche und Bedenken* (1927; *A*, 30–36), we find that Schnitzler occasionally poses the necessity of assuming free will and deprecates the consequences of irresponsible action. But as one peruses the numerous other aphorisms in the section, the preponderant emphasis on causality, destiny and the inevitable course of history becomes apparent. In any case, it does not seem that Schnitzler had as yet foresworn determinism in the years in which he conceived virtually all of the artists to whom we have referred: 1890–1910.

Now, in establishing a *positive* linkage between Schnitzler and his artists, it can be shown that he held the artist *per se* in high esteem. An admittedly late but nonetheless significant, non-fictional statement of this attitude may be found in the essay, *Der Geist im Wort und der Geist in der Tat* (1927), in which Schnitzler strove to evaluate "die *Beziehung* zwischen den *Urtypen* des menschlichen Geistes" (*A*, 136). Here the *Dichter* (who represents not only the literary artist but the creative personality in general) is highly regarded and placed virtually at the top of the scale. Above him stands only the prophet who is next to God. Under the *Dichter* on the one hand are the statesman, priest and politician, on the other the historian, philosopher and journalist. At the bottom of the scale, incidentally, we find the *Literat;* below him stands only the *Bösewicht* who is next to the devil.

In the essay Schnitzler obviously still holds to the view that the *Dichter* and the *Literat* are as different as day and night. Yet he finds that at times it is exceedingly difficult to distinguish between them and resorts to an unexpected moral yardstick. Flatly stating that the *Literat* can also create masterpieces, he defines the *Literat* as a narcissistic individual and the *Dichter* simply as "ein großer Mensch" (*A,* 151). Of the true artist, Schnitzler can still maintain, however: "Keiner ist so sehr wie er *Mensch von Gnaden des Augenblicks*" (*A,* 150).

The essay shows, then, despite some not insignificant changes of opinion, that Schnitzler still held the artist in the same high esteem implicit in his earlier writings. His long-abiding interest in the *Literat* is here also revealed for what it naturally had to be, a phase of his deep concern in the artist. The *Literat* was the reverse side of the coin, as it were.

Our hypothesis still faces a significant obstacle: the frequently expressed belief that the physicians among the author's characters are his true spokesmen. In a recent study,[15] Maria Alter has elucidated the complexity and multiplicity of Schnitzler's doctors and concluded that they fall into two basic groups, the "good" and the "bad" doctors, who, we might add, stand in a relationship comparable to that between the *Dichter* and the *Literat.* Taken as a whole, the good doctors are an admirable group of men who accept the Hippocratic oath as their personal ethic. What has not been widely recognized, however, is that even these good doctors have their weakness. Alter agrees on this point but believes the weakness to lie in a conflict between the physician and the man: "Stripped of literary distortions, the portrait of the Schnitzlerian physician appears inevitably two-faced: tilted toward the human side, it shows the ugly face of man; tilted toward the professional side, it shows a nonconformist idealist."[16] She believes in the case of Dr. Reumann, for example, that his life is a lie because he cannot reconcile "the primitive drive to assert his own interests" with an "acquired personality which dovetails with his medical conscience":

> But the greatest lie is Reumann's own life. No doubt, it is an admirable
> lie insofar as its altruism puts the welfare of others above one's own peace;

[15] Maria Alter, "Schnitzler's Physician: An Existential Character," *Modern Austrian Literature,* 4/3 (1971), 7–23.

[16] *Ibid.,* p. 18.

without that lie Reumann would not be a "good" physician; but its basic meaning remains unchanged by Schnitzler's approval: Reumann lives a role, wears a mask, hides his real self, dissimulates an unresolved conflict.[17]

We believe this interpretation to be in error. The conflict in Reumann is not so much between the man and the doctor as between conflicting aspects of his own real, not assumed, personality. Let us consider the situation briefly.

Reumann's problem has to do with Johanna Wegrat. He loves her deeply but cannot find the courage to declare himself. At the same time he cannot bring himself to leave, and turns down an excellent position in order to remain near Johanna; he feigns other reasons for staying, of course, but Johanna's mother Gabriele readily sees through this subterfuge. Bitterly, Reumann must watch, driven by desire on the one hand and damned to silence by his lack of self-assertiveness on the other, while Johanna directs her love to the aging artist, von Sala.

It is indefensible to imply that Reumann does not declare his love because it conflicts with his professional ethics. Marrying Johanna would in no way compromise his ethical code or his being a doctor, it reflects no conflict between doctor and man. One might say that his unassertive nature is one reason why he has become a doctor; he is a "born" doctor. His name Reumann—der Reuende—has ironic significance.

Similar ironic nomenclature with similar import is apparent also in the case of Dr. Mauer in *Das weite Land*. As Alter correctly states, he is "one of the most positive physicians in Schnitzler's writings."[18] But whereas she notes no weakness in Mauer, merely commenting that in his role there are few opportunities for action, the fact is, he, too, has a flaw. To be sure, this is no superficial weakness. Mauer is a good physician, a fine and upright man. The flaw is a purer version of Reumann's: he is the epitome of the good doctor.

What we mean becomes clear in the scene between Mauer and Erna, the girl he loves. Mauer is more aggressive than Reumann and is actively courting Erna in competition with the egotistical and dashing Hofreiter—a "good" doctor who clearly doesn't feel that marriage would conflict with his professional conscience. In a sense, Mauer has an advantage over Hofreiter in that he is proposing marriage. Moreover, he has the masculinity and brusque forthrightness of Schnitzler's strongest artists. Erna is well

[17] *Ibid.*
[18] *Ibid.*, p. 16.

aware of what he has to offer her and tells him so: "Sie sind wirklich ein anständiger Mensch, Doktor Mauer! Man hat so das Gefühl, wenn man Ihnen einmal sein Schicksal anvertraut . . . da ist man dann im Hafen. Da kann einem nichts mehr geschehn" (*DW* II, 253).

He is a good man. He would make a good husband. He offers security, a haven, a wall (*Mauer!*) against a hostile world. But Erna is not sure that security and goodness are the end-all of existence. She has an intuition that there are other values, perhaps higher, perhaps lower, that may be more meaningful:

> Nur weiß ich nicht recht, ob dieses Gefühl der Sicherheit etwas so besonders Wünschenswertes bedeutet. Wenigstens für mich. Wenn ich ganz auf- richtig sein soll, Doktor Mauer, mir ist manchmal, als hätt' ich vom Dasein auch noch andres zu erwarten oder zu fordern als Sicherheit—und Frieden. Besseres oder Schlimmeres—ich weiß nicht recht. (*DW* II, 253)

Ultimately Erna, characterized as an intelligent girl with character, decides in favor of a liaison with Hofreiter.

A similar evaluation of the doctor takes place in *Bacchusfest* (1915). Agnes is the wife of a gifted playwright, Felix Staufner. Not only does he leave home for weeks at a time to find the solitude necessary for his work, he is not above a romantic liaison on occasion. Piqued and lonely, Agnes, in turn, has an affair with Guido Wernig, a doctor—of chemistry, to be sure—but like the other "good" doctors, the essence of bourgeois virtue. He resembles Mauer in being masculine, reliable, conventional, possessive and a bit dull. To Agnes, who finds reliability at this point very gratifying in her loneliness, he seems an ideal person and she agrees to marry him. However, as they discuss their future life together, Agnes begins to sense what everyday life with Wernig will be like; he tells her that they will have a respectable household and that such questionable types as artists will never cross the threshold. When Felix joins them and Agnes has a chance to compare the two men, she quickly decides to stay with her husband. Living with the fickle and egotistical Felix may have its problems, but she finds it preferable to the dull respectability of life with Guido.

It is clear that even the best of Schnitzler's doctors are not the embodi- ment of human perfection and that the problem faced by Erna and Agnes is the author's own dilemma, which is present in so many of his plays. How nice it would be if all men were reliable and altruistic like Mauer, Reumann and Wernig. But such people are unfortunately also a bit dull and conven- tional. Their interest lies in such things as security—Nietzsche's "last man" comes to mind. Their personality forces them to forego the great experiences of life, "Besseres oder Schlimmeres," as Erna puts it, which are beyond the pale of conventional men.

This does not mean that Schnitzler totally rejected the doctor but that he views the latter as a type, with strengths and weaknesses, which is not unequivocally superior to the artist. It is interesting to note that in the aforementioned essay the doctor is rated highly but not quite as high as the *Dichter*. Whereas the *Dichter* was evaluated on a diagram entitled *Der Geist im Wort*, the doctor is relegated to the diagram *Der Geist in der Tat*. Here the doctor (= *Heilkünstler*) is two notches below the prophet, one notch lower than the *Dichter* on the other diagram. On the second diagram the hero stands directly below the prophet. But these details are admittedly trivial. What is important is that the diagrams show that Schnitzler viewed the ideal doctor and the ideal artist as noble human types—with the artist perhaps a shade nobler.

Hans Weigel summarizes Schnitzler's situation simply and accurately: "Was er gewesen war, stilisierte er als Anatol und Max, Fritz und Theodor."[19] Doctor-types and artist-types may be found in Schnitzler's earliest work and may be traced back to responsible chaps like Max and to aesthetes like Anatol. And as Weigel says, Schnitzler was never just the one or the other. He *was* the "Lebejüngling" Anatol, but he was *more* than that. He was also Max. The doctor in him always registered objections to the egotistical artist—this is apparent in all of his artist characterizations. But the artist in him, like the wolf in Hesse's *Steppenwolf*, constantly reminded him with rasping irony that bourgeois virtues did not lead to the essence of being.

We may now return to the three questions posed at the beginning of this chapter. As regards the first question, clearly all of Schnitzler's artists with their peculiar admixture of creativity, sensitivity, ruthlessness, egotism, and loneliness bear a close spiritual kinship to the creative and lonely superman in Nietzsche's *Thus Spake Zarathustra*, who eschews conventional morality and acts only in accordance with his own inner command. Consequently, the possibility of Nietzschean influence on Schnitzler's ethics is not to be ruled out. As for the second question, we have seen that Schnitzler thought highly of the artist; thus it should be obvious that his artists and artist-types must speak for him. With respect to the last question, what about the doctors? Obviously, they too, are spokes-

[19] In his introduction to *Liebe, die starb vor der Zeit* (Wien, 1970), p. 13.

men for the author, even though their views are often diametrically opposed to those of the artists. Here is perhaps the basic tension which underlies much of Schnitzler's writing. Like Faust, he had two souls within his breast. He saw life both through the eyes of the artist, egotistical and sensitive, and through the eyes of the unselfish doctor. For this reason Schnitzler in his writing occasionally did attack the egotistical artist whom, at such times, he viewed from the doctor's perspective. But it must not be forgotten that even the best among Schnitzler's doctors are characterized consistently as somewhat dull and lacking in imagination.

Few characters speak for the whole Schnitzler, but perhaps the last words of Heinrich Bermann in *Der Weg ins Freie* may be so interpreted:

> Ich hab mich ohne Schuld gefühlt. Irgendwo in meiner Seele. Und wo anders, tiefer vielleicht, hab ich mich schuldig gefühlt . . . und noch tiefer, wieder schuldlos. Es kommt immer nur darauf an, wie tief wir in uns hineinschauen. Und wenn die Lichter in allen Stockwerken angezündet sind, sind wir doch alles auf einmal: schuldig und unschuldig, Feiglinge und Helden, Narren und Weise. (*ES* I, 957)

For the aging Schnitzler, the dilemma is even better stated by his only lady genius, Marcolina in *Casanovas Heimfahrt*:

> Die Unendlichkeit und die Ewigkeit zu erfassen wird uns immer versagt sein; unser Weg geht von der Geburt zum Tode; was bleibt uns übrig, als nach dem Gesetz zu leben, das jedem von uns in die Brust gesenkt ist—oder auch wider das Gesetz? Denn Auflehnung wie Demut kommen gleichermaßen von Gott. (*ES* II, 280)

It may therefore be concluded that Nietzschean morality plays a pervasive role in the dialectic of Schnitzler's thought.

Nietzsche und Carl Sternheim

Seit über vier Jahrzehnten befaßt sich die Kritik mit der Frage, ob und wieweit Nietzsche auf den Dichter Carl Sternheim eingewirkt hat. Schon 1925 konstatierte Ludwig Marcuse eine Beziehung zwischen dem "Über-bürger" Sternheims und dem Gedankengut Nietzsches und Wedekinds.[1] Zehn Jahre später verstärkte Wolfgang Paulsen diese Auffassung in seinem Buch *Expressionismus und Aktivismus*.[2] Als Paulsen sich jedoch im Jahre 1956 mit Sternheim gründlich auseinandersetzte, wollte er nichts mehr "von einer unmittelbaren Abhängigkeit von Nietzsche" wissen.[3] George und Wedekind "seien die beiden Pole in Sternheims Dichtung."[4] Eher als zum Übermenschen wiesen die Helden Sternheims eine Verwandtschaft mit dem amerikanischen Typ des "rugged individual" auf.[5] In seinem 1960 herausgegebenen Buch über Georg Kaiser räumte Paulsen überraschender-weise die Möglichkeit einer Nietzsche-Beeinflussung wieder ein, fügte allerdings noch hinzu, daß Kaiser, Sternheim und andere expressionistische Dichter sich ihre Nietzsche-Kenntnisse "meist durch Osmose angeeignet" hätten.[6]

In seiner vorzüglichen Ausgabe des Sternheimschen Gesamtwerks (1963–1970) ordnete und bearbeitete Wilhelm Emrich viel neues Material, beschränkte sich aber im Vorwort hinsichtlich unsres Themas auf die Bemerkung, Sternheims Gedankengänge seien nicht neu und schon "von Stirner, Nietzsche, Bakunin, den sogenannten Anarchisten, zum Teil auch von heutigen Existentialisten geäußert" worden.[7] Wolfgang Wendler

---

[1] Ludwig Marcuse, "Das expressionistische Drama," *Literaturgeschichte der Gegenwart,* hrsg. Ludwig Marcuse (Berlin, 1925), II, 149–50.

[2] Wolfgang Paulsen, *Expressionismus und Aktivismus* (Bern und Leipzig, 1935), S. 76.

[3] Wolfgang Paulsen, "Carl Sternheim: Das Ende des Immoralismus," *Akzente*, 3 (1956), 278.

[4] a.a.O., S. 284.

[5] a.a.O., S. 278.

[6] Wolfgang Paulsen, *Georg Kaiser: Die Perspektiven seines Werkes* (Tübingen, 1960), S. 104.

[7] Carl Sternheim, *Gesamtwerk*, hrsg. von Wilhelm Emrich, 9 Bde. (Berlin, 1963–

andererseits hob 1966 gerade den Nietzsche-Einfluß mit der Schlußfolgerung wieder hervor, "Nietzsche ist also grundlegender als jeder andere für Sternheim wichtig gewesen."[8] Weil aber Wendler mit Paulsen einig war, daß sich "nirgends . . . ein tieferes Eindringen in Nietzsches Gedankengut belegen" läßt und weil er noch dazu überzeugt war, Nietzsches Einfluß beruhe "weniger auf einzelnen Gedanken, die Sternheim übernahm, als auf der Wirkung von Nietzsches Art zu denken," so ließ es Wendler bei einigen im ganzen zutreffenden aber allgemeinen Bemerkungen bewenden.[9]

Unsere Untersuchung wendet sich nochmals dem Problem Nietzsche —Sternheim zu, in der Überzeugung, es sei noch nicht gründlich erörtert worden. Obwohl wir den bedeutenden Studien von Paulsen und Wendler in vielem zustimmen, so meinen wir doch, den Einfluß Nietzsches etwas präziser bestimmen zu können. Dabei sind wir uns der ganzen Fragwürdigkeit des "Einfluß"-Begriffs bewußt: selten übernimmt der Mensch die Gedanken eines anderen, ohne sich selbst schon mehr oder weniger zu demselben Standpunkt durchgerungen zu haben.[10] Einfluß bzw. Wirkung kann aber auch so verstanden werden, daß man damit lediglich auf die schärfere Begriffsbildung hinsteuert, die einer Beschäftigung mit sympathischem Gedankengut entwächst.

Es geht uns nicht nur darum, Sternheim als Nietzsche-Anhänger darzustellen, sondern auch darum, die noch heftig umstrittene Weltanschauung Sternheims zu beleuchten. Verherrlichte er den Überbürger oder den Spießbürger? Sind seine Aussprüche, besonders die für die Öffentlichkeit bestimmten, eigentlich ernst zu nehmen? Soll man sein Denken als logisch oder nur als pathologisch betrachten?[11] Wir sehen den inneren Sinn

1970), Bd. 1, S. 9. Alle ferneren Hinweise auf das Werk Sternheims, den Roman *Europa* ausgenommen, beziehen sich auf diese Ausgabe. Zitatbelege werden in Klammern im Text direkt nach dem Zitat gegeben.

[8] Wolfgang Wendler, *Carl Sternheim* (Frankfurt am Main, 1966), S. 243. Überarbeitung seiner 1963 abgeschlossenen Dissertation.

[9] a.a.O., S. 243. Auch unterscheidet Wendler wenig zwischen den verschiedenen Phasen von Sternheims Nietzsche-Verhältnis, was ihn dazu verleitet im allgemeinen eine "zwiespältige Haltung" gegenüber Nietzsche bei Sternheim zu konstatieren, wobei dieser Nietzsche als Verkünder des "Willens zur Macht" ablehnt. Diese Schlußfolgerung gilt nur für den Nachkriegs-Sternheim.

[10] Zum Beispiel hatte Gottfried Keller sich schon zu dem Standpunkt einer gottlosen Naturordnung durchgerungen, als er im Jahre 1849 die Philosophie Ludwig Feuerbachs begeistert annahm.

[11] Winfried Georg Sebald, *Carl Sternheim* (Stuttgart, 1969), 146 S. Sebald findet Sternheim widersprüchlich, überschätzt und "weitgehend pathologisch" (S. 126).

dieser Arbeit darin, durch die Erörterung von Sternheims Beziehung zu Nietzsche zum besseren Verständnis Sternheims beizutragen.

In seinem Aufsatz über Sternheim schrieb Wolfgang Paulsen folgende Sätze:

> Auch in späteren Jahren scheint Sternheim sich niemals ernstlich mit Nietzsche und dem Phänomen des europäischen Immoralismus beschäftigt zu haben. Wo immer er auf Nietzsche zu sprechen kommt, hat er sich mit einigen hämischen und oft völlig verständnislosen Bemerkungen begnügt, wie das beinahe allen großen Namen der Weltgeschichte gegenüber seine Art war, aus dem Bedürfnis einer inneren Verteidigung heraus.[12]

Diese Aussage ist bisher noch unangefochten, und da wir ihr nicht ganz beipflichten, wollen wir zunächst Sternheims spätere, nach dem ersten Weltkrieg entstandene Schriften ins Auge fassen.[13]

Der im Jahre 1920 veröffentlichte Aufsatz, *Berlin oder Juste Milieu*, ist der bekannteste und dazu wohl auch der bedeutendste Sternheims aus dieser Zeit. Er hat dann auch den Ton fast sämtlicher kritischen Schriften in des Dichters Spätzeit bestimmt. Hier schildert Sternheim den geistigen Verfall Berlins in den Jahren 1870–1914 aus seiner Sicht. Die absolutistische Ordnung der preußischen Junker wurde durch die Weltanschauung Darwins abgelöst. Das Gefühl der persönlichen Verantwortlichkeit mußte "Naturnotwendigkeiten" weichen. "Masse" wurde Schlüsselwort. Dies führte zum Umbruch, zur Industrialisierung und zum Einzug einer Intelligenz aus dem Osten, die auf geistigem und schriftstellerischem Gebiet die Macht an sich riß. Statt aber nun eine neue und freie Weltanschauung zu bekunden, ließ diese Clique, die ihren eigenen Vorteil suchte und sich daher den führenden kapitalistischen Schichten eng verband, die alten Werte wieder aufleben.

Sternheim fand diese Entwicklung besonders tragisch, da der Umbruch die Möglichkeit eines geistigen und menschlichen Aufstiegs dargeboten hatte. Man hätte auf Nietzsche hören sollen:

[12] a.a.O., S. 282.

[13] Unseres Erachtens trifft Paulsens Vorwurf nur für Sternheims letzte größere Schrift, *Vorkriegseuropa im Gleichnis meines Lebens* (Amsterdam, 1936), zu. In dieser Zeit des aufkommenden nationalsozialistischen Deutschlands lehnte Sternheim Nietzsche entschieden ab. Die zwei diesbezüglichen Äußerungen in der Schrift *Vorkriegseuropa* lauten wie folgt: "Jeder war aus seiner praktischen Wirklichkeit der eigenen Gattung bewußt; wobei mit seinem hysterischen Übermenschen der spitzfindige Nietzsche nachhinkte" (S. 36); "Die Menschheit erlitt darüber hinaus Friedrich Nietzsches 'Willen zur Macht'; sein 'Jenseits von Gut und Böse.' Seines 'Übermenschen' Willkür übernahm die Führung der Welt!" (S. 122–23).

An sich hätte man sich denken können, die auf der Linie von Hegel und Haeckel gewachsene radikale Unverantwortlichkeit des Menschen vor Naturnotwendigkeiten sei bei dem Berliner und seinem ursprünglich unbekümmerten und bewußten Charakter in rechte Hände gekommen, er hätte, da er nichts mehr besorgen mußte, sich auf Grund der neuen Lehre wirklich grenzenloser Ausgelassenheit, jauchzender Lebenslust, etwa so prachtvoll und unvergleichlich hingegeben, wie ein einziger freier Deutscher, Nietzsche, es in diesem Augenblick zu fordern begann.

Es wäre denkbar gewesen, die in Deutschland am meisten verhätschelte Rasse der Berliner hätte sich solchen durch Philosophen rückversicherten Mut genommen, daß sie jenseits von Gut und Böse auf Grund großer Bankguthaben dionysische Laune, ein reines Lachen ausgetollt, ihre Landsleute, ganz Deutschland und schließlich abendländische Welt mit Lust angesteckt hätte.

Alle Umstände waren vollendet da. Nietzsche gab geistiges Geländer. (VI, 125)

1921 erschien die Schrift *Tasso oder die Kunst des Juste Milieu*, die im besonderen Goethe wegen seiner Verherrlichung von Pflicht und konventioneller Sittlichkeit stark rügte. Nochmals wird Nietzsche als potentieller Retter hervorgehoben:

Einen Augenblick schien es um des neunzehnten Jahrhunderts Ende, als könne das Goethesche "Leben und Leben-lassen" durch Friedrich Nietzsche bedroht, an des gemütlichen Tasso Stelle in deutscher Sehnsucht der rauhere Zarathustra treten. Als könne aus seiner Lehre statt sich entwickelnder besinnungsloser Hingabe an alle Welt der Deutsche einen brutalen Egoismus in vernünftiger Schöpfung entdecken, und ihn statt wie bisher verbrecherisch geradezu sittlich nennen.

Aber die wesentliche Kraft, die nach Nietzsches schnellem geistigem Erlöschen deutsches Geist- und Kunstleben in Ermangelung bedeutender deutscher Nachfolge am stärksten beeinflussen sollte, Henrik Ibsen, mußte beim Versuch, das robuste Nietzsche Gewissen in seinen Dramenhelden und -heldinnen durchzusetzen, alsbald einsehen, er habe sich in solchem Ziel übernommen. . . . (VI, 199)

Bemerkenswert ist, daß in beiden Aufsätzen, die im Abstand von einem Jahr erschienen sind, allein Nietzsche die rettende Kraft zugeschrieben wird. Obwohl Nietzsche in der Nachkriegszeit zum Modephilosophen wurde, ist die Bezugnahme nicht zufällig, wie im Laufe dieser Untersuchung noch zu zeigen ist. Nun fassen die Zitate den Kern der Nietzschelehre als "jauchzende Lebenslust" und "brutalen Egoismus" auf, was von einem gewissen Standpunkt aus noch vertretbar ist. Die Zitate weisen aber auch andere Momente auf, die schwerlich von Nietzsche herstammen könnten. Wie läßt sich das alles erklären? Am besten, wenn wir die ethische Auffassung Sternheims selbst, seine Theorie der Denk- und Beziehungsinhalte kurz überblicken.[14] Die ist sowohl im *Berlin*aufsatz wie in dem 1919 erschienenen Roman *Europa* enthalten.

Nach Sternheim gibt es eine absolute Gesetzmäßigkeit der "Naturnotwendigkeiten," der der Mensch gehorchen muß.[15] Er bekämpfte aber mit allen Mitteln die, wie er behauptete, vom *Juste Milieu* vertretene Ansicht, der Mensch habe sich auch einem objektiven Sittengesetz zu unterwerfen. Auf dem Gebiet der Beziehungsinhalte, meinte Sternheim, müsse der Mensch seine persönliche Freiheit, "seine eigene Nüance" bewahren:

> Diese zeitgenössische, momentane Welt aber besitzt der Mensch immer von neuem neu und unabhängig von Vernunft nur durch Kraft der *Vision* . . . . Und zwar nach seinen visionären Fähigkeiten in abgestuften Graden jeder andere Mensch immer anders, so daß auf diesem Gebiet der Beziehungen jeder historische Vergleich sinnlos ist. Erst durch diese individuell gestufte Möglichkeit zum immer verschiedenen Besitz des "Beziehungsganzen" ist der neugeborene Mensch mit einem eigenen unvergleichlichen Schicksal frei, das heißt ganz seine eigene Nüance! (VI, 170)

Die Beziehung zur Ethik Nietzsches liegt auf der Hand. Abweichende Momente, wie in den oben zitierten Auszügen, sind aber nicht zu verkennen. Diese wären 1. der Glaube an eine objektive Gesetzmäßigkeit, 2. die Bezugnahme nicht nur auf die wenigen Genies, sondern auf die ganze Menschheit, wobei allerdings eine Abstufung durch die "Kraft der Vision" des Einzelnen noch anerkannt wird,[16] 3. das Ziel der persönlichen Freiheit

---

[14] Die Anregung zu dieser etwas ungewöhnlichen Begriffsbildung ging vermutlich von Heinrich Rickert aus, der in seinem Werk, *Die Grenzen der naturwissenschaftlichen Begriffsbildung* (Freiburg, 1902), Denk-und Relationsbegriffe unterscheidet. Zu bemerken ist, daß es bei Rickert hauptsächlich um Metaphysisches, bei Sternheim vorwiegend um Ethisches geht.

[15] Sternheim scheint nie an der objektiven Wirklichkeit der sinnlichen Welt gezweifelt zu haben. Daher ist wohl sein mangelndes Interesse für Metaphysik zu erklären.

[16] "Kraft der Vision" ist eine durch den Krieg verursachte Abschwächung des früheren Sternheimschen Kraftbegriffs.

und des inneren Triebes sei weder die große Tat noch die Machtbereicherung, sondern der Lebensgenuß.[17]

Die abweichenden Momente sind also wesentlich dieselben wie in den Auszügen und es ist nun klar, worum es sich handelt. Die Nietzsche zugeschriebene Ethik trägt wohl Züge Nietzsches, ist aber im Grunde die Anschauung Sternheims. Das soll aber nicht gleich heißen, daß sich Sternheim gar nicht um Nietzsche bemüht oder sich nur eine oberflächliche Kenntnis von dessen Gedanken erworben hat. Wie noch zu zeigen ist, hat sich Sternheim Punkt für Punkt hinsichtlich dieser abweichenden Momente mit dem großen Immoralisten auseinandergesetzt. Er wußte also, daß das, was er hier Nietzsche unterschob, sein Eigenes war. Andererseits wußte er ebenso gut, wie eng seine eigene Meinung noch mit den Kerngedanken der Moral Nietzsches verwandt gewesen war; sie war so eng damit verwandt, daß er ohne Bedenken den Namen Nietzsches für seine eigene Version des Immoralismus einsetzen konnte.

Man muß es zugeben, in den Aufsätzen hat Sternheim die Moral Nietzsches zu eigenen Zwecken umgeformt. Es kann aber weder von "hämischen" noch von "verständnislosen Bemerkungen," sondern nur von einem ziemlich positiven, wenn auch bewußt distanzierten Verhältnis zu Nietzsche und zu dessen Ethik die Rede sein. Diese Ansicht findet ihre volle Bestätigung in dem fast gleichzeitig veröffentlichten Roman *Europa*.[18]

Ehe wir uns aber von den *Juste-Milieu*-Schriften abwenden, soll noch kurz darauf hingewiesen werden, wie sehr sie von Ausdrücken und Gedanken des Zarathustra-Dichters Gebrauch machen. Einige Beispiele mögen genügen. "Leben" wird mit dem "zum Gesetz Erstarrten" verglichen (VI, 189). "Hegelsche Verkündigung" werde durch das *Juste Milieu* "völlig zu Pöbelinstinkten und Pöbelwerten" degradiert (VI, 194). Der "Mitleidsbefehl nicht nur Hegels aber auch Schopenhauers und Wagners" wird negativ bewertet (VI, 197). Vorwurfsvoll spricht man von "Aufzucht zum Herdenvolk" (VI, 133). Wie Nietzsche "Sklavenmoral" aus dem Ressentiment der Schwachen herleitet, so meint Sternheim vom "jüdischen Berliner": "in ihr (der Presse) konnte er anonym sein Ressentiment gegen alles Heilige und Höchstpersönliche austoben" (VI, 132). "Begriffe, die

---

[17] Wie Richard Dehmel, Frank Wedekind und der junge Heinrich Mann beschränkte Sternheim den "Lebenstrieb" vielfach auf den "Geschlechtstrieb."

[18] Carl Sternheim, *Europa* (München, 1919), 2 Bde. Weitere Hinweise auf diesen Roman beziehen sich auf diese Ausgabe und werden im Text angeführt.

einseitig nach sittlichem Dienst messen" findet Sternheim "lebensschwächend" (VI, 140). Dem Bürger soll "Mut zu seiner menschlichen Ursprünglichkeit," "Mut zu seinen sogenannten Lastern" gemacht werden (VI, 140). "Allmächtig lebendige, brutale Lebensfrische" wird "verblasenen Theorien" gegenüber gestellt (VI, 140). "Daß Kraft sich nicht verliert, muß . . . auf seinen frischen Einzelton der Mensch nur hören, unbesorgt darum, wie Bürgersinn seine manchmal brutale Nuance nennt" (VI, 139).

Der Roman *Europa* (1919) behandelt dasselbe Phänomen des europäischen Zusammenbruchs und kommt zu ähnlichen Ergebnissen. Maßgeblicher Sprecher des Autors ist der Dichter Carl Wundt, der seine revolutionäre und heilbringende Botschaft—man spricht von "einem so riesigen, seit Jahrhunderten unvergleichlichen Geschenk an Deutsche" (I, 177)—in Form einer Erzählung bekannt gibt. Der anpassungssüchtige Wolf Schwarzenberg, unbekannter Herkunft, bisher von Ressentiment getrieben (I, 141), verliebt sich in ein Mädchen aus dem Rheinland. Seiner selbst nicht sicher, versucht er sich ganz der rheinländischen Kultur zu bemächtigen und sich den rheinländischen Menschen anzupassen. Diese Selbstverleugnung gelingt ihm in hohem Maße. Fast wie ein Wunder nun erscheint eines Tages die Heißgeliebte, von allen Vorurteilen befreit, und schenkt sich ihm. Von Glück überwältigt, kann sich Wolf aber nun nicht mehr von seiner neuangenommenen bürgerlichen Persönlichkeit befreien. Er hat sich von seiner Ursprünglichkeit zu weit entfernt, um jetzt noch das Leben der bürgerlichen Sicherheit vorzuziehen. Auf leisen Sohlen entfernt er sich von der schlafenden, lebensfrischen Eva, um zu der nicht vitalen, aber bürgerlich anerkannten Professorentochter zurückzukehren.

Es fällt natürlich sofort auf, wie sehr Wundts Erzählung die uns nun bekannte Ethik Sternheims verkörpert. Dazu wird Wundt mit seinem Schöpfer geradezu identifiziert. Wie dieser hat auch er ein *Don-Juan*-Drama verfaßt (II, 69), das "in Berlin zu beispiellosem Theaterskandal geführt" hat (I, 98). Wie Sternheim sich auch eben nicht unterschätzte, so wird Wundt von den beiden anderen Hauptpersonen im Roman, Eura und Rank, für den größten deutschen Dichter der modernen Zeit gehalten (II, 69).

Wie verhält sich Wundt—Sternheim zu Nietzsche? Grundsätzlich bejahend. Als zum Beispiel Wolf seinen großen Fehler der Selbstverleugnung begeht, deutet dies Wundt symbolisch dadurch an, daß er Wolf die männliche Lektüre von Nietzsche, Marx und Bakunin gegen die konventionelleren Texte von Schiller und Kleist eintauschen läßt:

Nun zügelte er und vergewaltigte in sich Gewalten, die er aufge-peitscht hatte, verabscheute Musik, wie sie chaotisch in seinen Abgründen brauste, floh vor Urwald und Dickicht in sich; erbleichte Marx und Nietzsche zu kennen, verwünschte ihre finsteren Sprüche, schleuderte seinen Bakunin in die Ecke. Mochte Bier und Branntwein nicht mehr und verbrachte über Schillers und Kleists Lektüre in Konditoreien Freizeit. (I, 142)

Wundt verhöhnt Goethe als "pünktlichen Niederschlag mittelrheinischer Poeterei: höchstens angemessen versonnen, niemals entrückt," während er Nietzsche indirekt lobt: "Hier hatte überstürzte Aufklärung, kein Mysti-zismus und nichts Dämonisches Platz gehabt; hier war kein Huß und Nietzsche geboren. Hier diente man lebendigen Interessen und verdient" (I, 150). Goethe als Spießbürger wird dem ins Dämonische gesteigerten Nietzsche recht negativ gegenübergestellt.

Am Anfang des Romans betrachtet Wundt die Welt mit einem Anflug des Nietzscheschen Nihilismus. Das grauenhafte Dasein, das Allzumensch-liche, erträgt er nur, indem er es verabscheut: "Denn grauenhaftes Dasein trage er nur durch die Sprengkraft tödlicher Abneigung gegen Allzu-menschliches um ihn," (I, 40). Gegen Ende des Buches erreicht er den urteilslosen *Amor fati* Nietzsches, freilich mit leicht religiösem Anstrich. Seiner Freundin Eura teilt er mit, seine bejahende Haltung trotz der vielen Schlechtigkeiten in der Welt "sei kein Werturteil, sondern, wie er ihr schon oft bedeutet habe, Aufforderung zu freierem und heftigerem Genuß der Welt" (II, 126). Diese Ansicht entstamme der Haltung: "Neugier und darüber hinaus beruhigte Unterwerfung unter von Gott gewollte kernige Wirklichkeit" (II, 126). Solche "kernige Wirklichkeit" bezieht sich in diesem Kontext auf das Harte, Brutale, also auf das Böse, oder besser gesagt, auf den Bereich jenseits von Gut und Böse. Freie Bejahung im Angesicht der rauhen Wirklichkeit entspricht dem Sinn des *Amor fati*. Wundt mag Nietzsche und denkt in vielem wie er. Nur vom "Willen zur Macht," den er nun streng vom Lebenstrieb unterscheidet, will Wundt nichts hören. Er schließt seine Diskussion der Beziehungsinhalte mit dem Ruf, "Aufbruch vom Willen zur Macht zum Trieb reinen Lebens hin" (II, 214). Vom Begriff "Wille zur Macht" distanziert sich Wundt-Stern-heim, da er nach dem Krieg die fatale Entwicklung Europas und besonders Deutschlands diesem Triebe zuschreibt:

Instinktiv wird Europa seit Jahrhunderten, bewußt seit über hundert Jahren von diesem einzigen Drang nach Wirksamkeit, Tat, Fortschritt und seinem Ziel, Kapital vergewaltigt, und was letzte Jahrzehnte hinzubrachten, war nur dieses Willens zur Macht schnelleres Tempo. . . . Und gerade der Deutsche. Nie und nirgends, in keinem Wort, keiner Führergeste fiel ihm ein, deutschen Machtwillens, Geschäfts Methoden [sic] auf ihren geistigen Gehalt zu prüfen, sondern von Anfang an hat er dieses Freibeutertum akzeptiert . . . (II, 212–13)

Dieser "Wille zur Macht," der zum Krieg führte, zeige sich schon wieder in der russischen "Diktatur des Proletariats" (I, 215). Deswegen wendet sich Wundt vom schnellen Tempo des "Willens zur Macht," zum ruhigen Beharren bei sich selbst: "Nicht Wettlauf zum Ziel, das keins ist, kein Äußerstes von Aktivität, doch ein Verweilen, Beharren bei sich selbst und jeder Regung der Umwelt" (II, 213). Von Nietzsche beeinflußte Terminologie ist auch hier wieder reichlich vorhanden, doch wollen wir aus räumlichen Gründen von einer diesbezüglichen Erläuterung absehen und statt dessen kurz darauf hinweisen, wie sehr die Hauptgestalten Wundt und Eura als Übermenschen aufgefaßt werden. Eura ist "ein Artgipfel": "Wie Kohinor und Großmogul sei sie für alle Zeit weiblicher Geltung Solitär, aus dem Schopf rotgoldener Flechten höchste Nuance, irgend ein Artgipfel, nach dem ein über die Welt versprengter Klüngel von Männern wallfahren, und vor dem er sich immer erniedrigen werde" (I, 18). Symbolisch gesehen stellt Eura den europäischen Sozialismus dar, als Frau vertritt sie den vitalen Lebenstrieb. In ihrer Verbindung von Kunstgefühl, politischem Idealismus und ungehemmter Sinnlichkeit erinnert sie eher an Heinrich Manns Herzogin von Assy als an Wedekinds Lulu oder Georg Kaisers Judith. Wie es fast immer der Fall bei Sternheim ist, wird jedoch urgründige Lebenskraft der Sinnlichkeit gleichgesetzt. Noch im blutigen Sterben will Eura die Wollust kulminieren: "Wollust ein letztes Mal zu kulminieren, greift sie den Soldatenstiefel, der steil in ihren Unterleib fährt, zieht ihn tief in zuckende Gedärme und entblättert . . ." (II, 220).

Wundt steht auf noch höherer Ebene. Wie Eura besitzt er eine ungeheuere Vitalität, "eine Lebenskraft . . . die sie (Eura) packte und wie mit Düften der Dschungel berauschte" (I, 39). Von ihm allein ist dann auch die geistige Rettung Europas zu erwarten (II, 178).

Wie Wundt schätzt auch Eura Nietzsche. Wenn sie ihn als Vorkämpfer des Sozialismus bewundert, stimmt ihr Sternheim wohl zu: "In diesem weiteren Sinn, nicht als Selbstzweck schätzte sie Nietzsche, des Vorkämpfers und seines Jüngers Bergsons Philosophien . . ." (II, 154).[19] Als

---

[19] Rickert im Vorwort zur revidierten Ausgabe seines Buches (s. Anm. 14) bezieht sich hinsichtlich der neueren Philosophie gerade auf Nietzsche und Bergson. Es mag sein, daß er dies dann auch in den Vorlesungen getan hat, die Sternheim besuchte.

verblendeter Sozialistin mangelt ihr aber Wundts Scharfsinn, so wird uns angedeutet, und mit Sternheim müssen wir vorwurfsvoll erkennen, wie sie im Gegensatz zu Wundt den "epochalen Trieb zur Expansion," wovon "Nietzsches Wille zur Macht" die letzte Phase sei, freudig begrüßt (II, 30). Fassen wir zusammen: der Roman *Europa* bezeugt wieder die Nachkriegs-Distanzierung Sternheims von Nietzsche. Gleichzeitig ist nicht zu übersehen, wie sehr der Roman in seiner Gesamtheit eine Auseinandersetzung mit Nietzsche darstellt, wobei Sternheim den Immoralisten hoch einschätzt und im wesentlichen bejaht.

Die intensive Beschäftigung Sternheims mit Nietzsche in den Nachkriegsjahren mag zum Teil auf seine während des Krieges begonnenen Freundschaft mit dem Dichter und damaligen Militärarzt Gottfried Benn zurückzuführen sein, denn Benn war ein Nietzsche-Enthusiast, der sich noch nach dem zweiten Weltkrieg mutig zu Nietzsche bekannte. Sternheims Interesse mag auch vom Zeitgeist angeregt worden sein, so wie es bei Hermann Hesse der Fall war. Jedenfalls aber war dies nicht die erste Begegnung mit Nietzsche.

In ihrer Konzeption umfassen die Komödien *Aus dem bürgerlichen Heldenleben* das zweite Jahrzehnt des 20. Jahrhunderts. Und wenn auch das erste Stück nicht 1908, wie Sternheim angab, sondern erst 1909 geschrieben worden ist, und wenn die letzten Stücke zum Teil neue Themen aufweisen, so stimmt doch im wesentlichen seine Behauptung, daß die Stücke eine innere Einheit haben. Es läßt sich also dieser Zeitabschnitt in Sternheims Schaffen durch eine Analyse des ersten Stücks, *Die Hose*, das dann auch die gedankliche Grundlage der weiteren Stücke darstellt, gut ins Auge fassen.

Die Handlung des Dramas scheint auf den ersten Blick wenig Gemeinsamkeiten mit Nietzsche zu zeigen. Eine junge Frau verliert unversehens ihre Schlupfhose auf der Straße. Ihr Mann, körperlich robust, aber im Beruf nur kleiner Beamter, ist entsetzt und fürchtet dadurch seine Stelle zu verlieren. Zwei männliche Zeugen des Ereignisses verlieben sich in die Frau und wollen den Mann zum Hahnrei machen. Wie er nun die Sache für sich zum Besten wendet, ist Kern der Handlung und des Humors. In dem Kampf des Gatten mit den zwei Verliebten geht es äußerlich um die Frau. Auf einer höheren Ebene geht es um Nietzsche.

Der eine Verliebte heißt Scarron und ist Dichter. Er ist ein Verehrer Nietzsches. Im dritten Akt fragt er den Gatten, Theobald Maske, "Ist Ihnen der Name Nietzsches zu Ohren gekommen?" (I, 87). Als Maske dann (fast wie Hesses Peter Camenzind) nur ein erstauntes "Wieso?" hervorbringen kann, summiert Scarron die Ethik Nietzsches: "Er lehrt das Evangelium der Zeit. Durch das mit Energie begnadete Individuum, kommt Ziel in die unübersehbare Masse der Menschen. Kraft ist höchstes Glück" (I, 87). In einer früheren Fassung des Dramas äußerte sich Scarron weitläufiger:

> Er lehrt das Evangelium des begnadeten Individuums. Durch ihn erst kommt System in die unübersehbare Masse der Menschen, in die er das Prinzip des aus sich selbst gearteteten Menschen, den Einser unter Nullen setzt ... Und diese Philosophie erdachte nicht etwa graue Theorie, sondern die Wirklichkeit hat sie gelehrt und lehrt sie allenthalben jeden Tag. Wem ist das Gleichnis vom Maulwurfsweibchen unbekannt, das von der Schar der um sie streitenden Männchen in die letzte unentrinnbare Ecke des letzten Ganges gedrückt wird und dort dem übrigbleibenden zufällt. Ist es bei den Bären oder bei den Menschen anders? (VII, 854–55)

In der frühen Fassung stimmt ihm Theobald nur bedingt zu: "Glück ist bei den Weibern halt auch dabei" (VII, 855). Worauf Scarron die klischeehafte Antwort gibt: "Aber was heißt das? Kraft ist Glück" (VII, 855).

Damit ist der Dialog zwischen Maske und Scarron eingeleitet. In der endgültigen Fassung geht das weniger schnell. Zunächst willigt Theobald vorsichtig ein, "Kraft ist freilich Glück. Das wußte ich auf der Schule, hatten die andern unter mir zu leiden" (I, 87). Worauf aber Scarron eine gewichtige Unterscheidung macht: "Natürlich meine ich nicht brutale Körperkräfte. Vor allem geistige Energien" (I, 87). Einige Minuten später greift Scarron den ausweichenden Theobald wieder an: "Hörten Sie von diesen Theorien nie sprechen? Lesen Sie so wenig?" (I, 88). Scarron wirft ihm Bequemlichkeit vor, worauf Theobald, endlich ein wenig aufgebracht, reagiert: "Ist bequem nicht recht? Mein Leben währet siebenzig Jahre. Auf dem Boden des mir angelernten Bewußtseins kann ich manches in diesem Zeitraum auf meine Weise genießen" (I, 90). Das genügt Scarron nicht. Nicht Genuß, sondern Mitarbeit an der geistigen Entwicklung des Menschengeschlechts sei das Maßgebende: "Ich beurteile den Mann einfach nach dem Grad seiner Mitarbeit an der geistigen Entwicklung des Menschengeschlechts. Heroen sind die großen Denker, Dichter, Maler, Musiker. Der Laie so bedeutend, wie weit er sie kennt" (I, 90). Worauf der zweite Verliebte, der schwindsüchtige Friseur und Wagner-Schwärmer Mandelstam, ihm begeistert zustimmt: "Und die großen Erfinder" (I, 90).[20]

---

[20] Wie sehr Mandelstam in geistiger Hinsicht zu Scarron hält, läßt sich aus seiner Verteidigung Scarrons gegenüber Luise ersehen. Mit Theobald verglichen sei "Herr Scarron wie der liebe Gott." Scarron bewies "Vornehmheit der Gesinnung." Er hatte "ein großes überströmendes Herz." Es war "rührend, wie er noch am späten Abend versuchen [wollte], Aufklärung in diesen Wasserkopf [Theobald] zu gießen" (I, 99).

Nun bringt Theobald den Einwand hervor, der in der ersten Fassung viel früher erscheint: "Und wo bleiben Sie mit dem Gemüt? . . . Wie brauchen Sie das Herz dazu?" (I, 91). Auf Scarrons kaltblütige Bemerkung, "Das Herz ist eine Muskel, Maske" (I, 91), erwidert Theobald, "Gut. Doch es hat eine Bewandtnis bei ihm. Bei den Weibern vor allem" (I, 91).

Scarron und Mandelstam bemühen sich, ihm zu beweisen, daß große Geister—Shakespeare, Goethe, Schwarz, Newton—bei ihren Errungenschaften nicht an Frauen gedacht hatten (I, 91), jedoch Theobald wird nicht überzeugt: "Von Goethe zu schweigen, meinetwegen von Schwarz—immerhin—um mich so auszudrücken, die Weiber haben ihr Herz" (I, 91). Dies Gespräch wird einige Seiten weitergeführt, bis Theobald seine Meinung etwas eindeutiger zu verstehen gibt: "Nun gibt es aber Wesen, für die ist ein Platz wie der andere, und vor allem mögen sie den, an dem sie stehen. Mit dem, was mir Geburt beschieden, bin ich an meinem Platz in günstiger Lage . . ." (I, 96). Der verblüffte Scarron kann nur erwidern, ". . . Sklavenmoral!" Theobald aber grinst und gibt seiner Weisheit letzten Schluß kund: "Meine Freiheit ist mir verloren, achtet die Welt auf mich in besonderer Weise. Meine Unscheinbarkeit ist die Tarnkappe, unter der ich meinen Meinungen, meiner innersten Natur frönen darf" (I, 96). Da sind die Fronten gezogen. In der darauffolgenden Handlung siegt Theobald auf ganzer Linie. Die Verliebten mieten teure Zimmer bei ihm, ohne an die schöne Luise zu gelangen, während Theobald genügend Kapital aus den lüsternen Untermietern schlägt, um sich eine Mätresse zulegen und eine Familie gründen zu können. Scarron rettet sich zwar zur Nietzsche-Moral zurück, entwickelt sich aber dabei zur Karikatur. Erst die Keuschheit einer Straßendirne läßt ihn wieder an die Relativität der Werte glauben:

> . . . nie vorher im Umgang mit Kindern und der Madonna war Keuschheit mit solcher Inbrunst wie aus dieser Hure mir nah. Und alsbald merke ich: Ihr [Theobalds] mit Emphase vorher ausgesagtes Urteil von der Unveränderlichkeit aller Werte—das nämlich ist der platte Sinn ihrer Lebensauffassung . . . ungültig wurde es vor diesem Weib . . . (I, 126)

Wir haben diese lange Auseinandersetzung Sternheims mit der Moral Nietzsches in allen Einzelheiten wiedergegeben, um einmal ihre außerordentliche Bedeutung für das Stück hervorzuheben, sodann aber auch, weil sie nicht ohne weiteres verständlich ist. Aber wie ist sie zu erklären?

Es fällt auf, daß beide Nietzsche-Verehrer Schwächlinge sind. Mandelstam kann sich eigentlich nichts Höheres denken, als abends allein mit Luise den *Fliegenden Holländer* zu lesen (I, 70). Scarron versteht sich zwar als harten Übermenschen. Als Mandelstam ihm bei seiner Werbung um Luise im Wege zu stehen droht, schnauzt er, "Herrenmoral soll dem schlappen Hund gezeigt werden" (I, 90). Auf Luisens Frage, ob "kein Mitleid mehr sein soll," antwortet er barsch, "ist einfach nicht" (I, 90). Er findet "unvergleichliche Wohltat in dem Gedanken: das Schwache, Lebensunfähige, muß dem Starken, Gesunden weichen" (I, 86). Trotz aller atavistisch klingenden Nietzscheterminologie ist und bleibt Scarron ein großmäuliger Schwärmer mit schwachen Trieben. Dies zeigt sich dann auch eindeutig, als er stürmisch um Luise wirbt. In dem Augenblick, wo sie sich endlich völlig bereitwillig zeigt, verläßt er sie, läuft glücklich in sein eigenes Zimmer und schließt ab, um das Erlebnis auf Papier zu verewigen.[21]

Scarron ist also ein Großmaul und Schwächling. Warum hat ihn dann Sternheim zum Fürsprecher Nietzsches gemacht? Offenbar, um sich schon zu diesem Zeitpunkt von Nietzsche zu distanzieren. In einem wichtigen Punkt aber unterscheidet sich diese Distanzierung ganz wesentlich von der späteren. Denn hier geht es nicht um eine Verneinung, sondern um eine Bejahung der Kraft.

Es soll nochmals darauf hingewiesen werden, daß Theobald die ursprüngliche Erläuterung der Moral Nietzsches als Sieg des Starken durch Scarron nicht ganz abgelehnt hat. Nur wollte er die Kraft nicht lediglich als geistige Energie aufgefaßt haben, die Starken nicht nur in den geistigen Menschen sehen. Er unterscheidet sich in dieser Hinsicht von Scarron nur insofern, als er die Kraft in den Bereich des Alltäglichen verlegt. Theobald zufolge hat jeder Mensch die Möglichkeit sowie das Recht, sich jenseits von Gut und Böse zu verhalten. Zwar komme es schon auf die Kraft jedes einzelnen an, auch gibt es keinen unbedingten Spielraum, innerhalb gewisser Grenzen aber könne sich jeder bemühen, seine persönliche Freiheit zu wahren, seinen inneren Trieben zu frönen.

Obwohl Theobald es nicht ausdrücklich erwähnt, setzt er die Vitalität fast ausschließlich der Geschlechtskraft gleich. Durch die wiederholte Betonung der eigenen starken Muskulatur will er die abgeschwächte Männlichkeit Mandelstams hervorheben. Nicht "Mitarbeit an der geistigen Entwicklung des Menschengeschlechts," sondern "Genuß" ist ihm Lebensziel. Wie sehr er dieses Lebensziel erotisch auffaßt, ist beim Fallen des Vorhangs klar: er schätzt sich mehr als glücklich, da er in zweifacher

---

[21] Scarrons übersteigerter Wunsch, das Erlebnis auf Papier zu verewigen, soll vermutlich eine Ironisierung Goethes sein. In seiner Tasso-Schrift wirft Sternheim denn Goethe auch vor, keine ergreifenden Verhältnisse mit Frauen gehabt zu haben (VI, 191).

Hinsicht auf dem Gebiet des Sexuellen Fortschritte erzielt hat: er hat eine Mätresse gewonnen, und, finanziell gesehen, kann er sich nun auch Kinder leisten.[22]

Theobalds auf dem Kraftbegriff basierende Immoralität wird dann zur Grundlage der weiteren Stücke *Aus dem bürgerlichen Heldenleben.* Möge die Bemerkung des alternden Theobald gegenüber seinem Sohn Christian in dem 1913 geschriebenen Stück, *Der Snob*, uns hier genügen: "In dir ist alles Maskesche um ein paar Löcher weitergeschnallt. Du hast mich völlig in dir . . . Meine Beziehung zur Welt, der höhere Sinn von mir—bist du" (I, 201). Fassen wir wieder zusammen: in der Komödie *Die Hose*, und somit indirekt auch in den damit verwandten Stücken, distanziert sich Sternheim bewußt von Nietzsche hinsichtlich seines Geniemenschen, seiner Zielsetzung, seiner Geringschätzung der Frauen, auch hinsichtlich seines Kraftbegriffs. Trotzdem steht er in der Bejahung einer auf Kraft gegründeten Immoralität Nietzsche näher als in der Nachkriegszeit, wo er ihn auch gelegentlich recht positiv bewertet hat. Obwohl Sternheim die Geniemoral Nietzsches, wie sie Scarron zum Ausdruck brachte, abgelehnt hat, so ist nichtsdestoweniger die Kraftethik Theobald Maskes auf Nietzsche zurückzuführen. Das wollen wir nun zu zeigen versuchen, indem wir die vermutlich entscheidende Begegnung Sternheims mit Nietzsche während der Konzeption des *Don Juan* erörtern.

Es besteht wenig Zweifel darüber, daß *Don Juan* weltanschaulich für Sternheim von größter Bedeutung gewesen war. Emrich meint, das Stück sei von allen vor der *Hose* "das Gewichtigste" gewesen (VII, 850). Er behauptet sogar, "das Stück wurde Sternheim mehr und mehr zu einer Summe seiner Existenz" (VII, 808). Sternheim selbst schrieb Mai 1906, "Am Don Juan, wie es recht ist und billig, erlebe ich mein ganzes Leben" (VII, 842).

Das Drama besteht aus zwei Teilen. Der erste Teil wurde im Juni 1905

---

[22] Die Kritik irrt, wenn sie meint, Sternheim habe sich auch von Theobald Maske distanziert. Bei ihm ist keine Karikierung anzutreffen. Wenn er auch am Anfang in seiner Angst Luise anschnauzt und sogar schlägt, so läßt Sternheim trotzdem durchschimmern, daß dieser Mann der einzige ist, der seine Frau wirklich versteht, der sie nicht wie Scarron fälschlich idealisiert, sondern sie nimmt, wie sie ist, als das Kind der Schneidersleute. Es darf auch nicht übersehen werden, daß Theobald eben derjenige ist, der Herz, Gemüt, und die Bedeutung des weiblichen Geschlechts in Schutz nimmt. Was man auch von ihm halten mag, Maske denkt und fühlt in vielem wie sein Schöpfer. Sternheims Diener meinte dann auch in Theobald Sternheim selbst zu sehen. Manche gestrichenen, von Emrich wiedergegebenen Aussagen Theobalds lauten fast wie "ein Glaubensbekenntnis . . . Sternheims" (I, 566).

geschrieben und im November desselben Jahres umgearbeitet. Erst bei der Umarbeitung kam Sternheim der Gedanke, noch einen zweiten Teil hinzuzufügen, der dann Herbst 1906 angefangen wurde.

Es ist nun auffallend, wie sehr die beiden Teile in der Konzeption des Helden voneinander abweichen. Nimmt man die Pläne zum zweiten Teil hinzu, so wird der Unterschied noch erheblicher.

Im ersten Teil hat man es mit einer Liebesgeschichte zu tun, wobei der egoistische und von Liebessehnsucht gequälte Held nicht ganz zufällig an Goethes Faust erinnert. Im zweiten Teil spielt die Liebe eine untergeordnete Rolle. Die Geliebte begeht bald Selbstmord, und die Handlung konzentriert sich darauf, Don Juan als großen Kriegsführer und Gegenspieler des Königs darzustellen.

Dieser Wandel vom Liebhaber zum selbstsicheren Weltmann läßt sich ja auch in *Faust* vorfinden. Es steht aber mehr auf dem Spiel. Das ergibt sich am deutlichsten aus den Briefen Sternheims an seine Freundin und spätere Frau, Thea Löwenstein-Bauer. Noch im Januar 1906 bezieht sich Sternheim auf Schiller und versteht den Kampf zwischen Don Juan und König Philipp als den zwischen zwei fast ebenbürtigen Gegnern (VII, 834). Dagegen zeigt ein im Februar desselben Jahres geschriebener Brief eine überraschende Neuerung. Sternheim beteuert, einen großen Fehler begangen zu haben: Don Juan sei als die Kraft, als Machthaber des Lebens, anzusehen, während Philipp als haßerfüllter, ohnmächtiger Schwächling zu betrachten sei:

> . . . Den großen Fehler habe ich am . . . Januar gemacht, als mir der wahnsinnige Vergleich Juan—Quichotte kam. . . . Es ist alles reiner Mist . . . es ist ein Irrtum von uns anzunehmen, Juan sei die Sehnsucht. Er ist die *Kraft*. . . . *Er ist der Machthaber des Lebens*, der Mächtige aus sich, der Sonnengott. Der König! das Plus! *Philipp, der König ist der ohnmächtige*, das Minus, die Schwäche an sich. Der Unterthan. Der Abhängige.
> . . . Schwäche. Kraft.
> Schatten. Sonne.
> Das ist der Konflikt. Darum haßt Philipp.
> . . . Die ohnmächtige Macht Philipps, die versucht diese Sonne zu erlöschen . . . ist zu zeigen. Zu zeigen die Lebensfülle . . . *Ein Wunder des Lebens ist zu zeigen*, der Lebenskraft. (VII, 838–39)

Von Schiller zu Nietzsche! Der Konflikt wird plötzlich im Sinne von Nietzsches Herrenmoral aufgefaßt! Der Starke handelt aus Lebensfülle und Kraft, der Schwache aus Ohnmacht und Ressentiment—"Philipp verkörpert eben diese Welt herrlich, der das wahrhaft große Starke verhaßt, gefürchtet . . . ist" (VII, 840). Woher der Wandel? Was bestimmte diesen Umschwung?

Ein zweiter Brief Sternheims von Februar 1906, aus der Zeit des Umschwungs also, berichtet von einem neuen philosophischen Interesse: "Ich habe mich vorsichtig mit Windelbands vorzüglicher Geschichte der Philosophie auf diese eingelassen und habe unendliche Freude (obwohl es mir sehr schwer fällt) damit, kann es nicht mehr ertragen, die Philosophie als die Wissenschaft, die uns Erkenntnisse, d.i. *Werturteile* über die Fragen der Ethik und Aesthetik vor allem giebt, zu entbehren" (VI, 473). Ein dritter Brief des Monats verrät die fortgesetzte Beschäftigung mit dem Problem des ethischen Verhaltens. Sternheim ringt bewußt darum, die persönliche Entschlußkraft zu bewahren, sein ganzes Denken aber steht noch im traditionellen Geleise: "Ein ethischer Mensch thut, was ihm seine beste Einsicht, *sein* höchstes Pflichtbewußtsein vorschreibt, nicht wie unethische, was ihm eine landläufige Moral, faule Prinzipien befehlen. . . . Der ethische Mensch . . . untersucht *in jedem Falle, was ist meine* Pflicht. Und läßt sich dann *ohne Rücksicht auf seine Neigung*, einzig von seiner Pflicht leiten . . ." (VI, 473–74). Sternheim unterscheidet scharf zwischen Pflicht und "landläufiger Moral," schließt aber ganz im Sinne Kants und des deutschen Idealismus: "Ich füge noch einmal ausdrücklich hinzu. *Pflicht*, nicht *Neigung*. Einsicht!" (VI, 474).

Ende Februar kehrte Sternheim aus Rom nach Freiburg zurück, wo er bei dem Schüler Windelbands, dem Universitätsprofessor Heinrich Rickert, Vorlesungen über Ethik hörte. Daß er in manchem mit Rickert nicht übereinstimmte, bezeugt ein an diesen gerichteter Brief vom 27. November 1906, in dem er Rickerts Auffassung vom großen künstlerischen Menschen stark ablehnt (VI, 484). Im selben Monat schreibt er begeistert über Nietzsche und seine Ethik: "Eine Milde. Etwa mit Nietzsche zu sagen: Es wäre entsetzlich, wenn wir noch an die Sünde glaubten, sondern, was wir auch tun werden—es ist unschuldig. Ich weiß wohl, daß der Don Juan Kraft ist vom Anfang bis zum Ende . . ." (VII, 847). Daraufhin zitiert er Nietzsche (Nachlaß, GA XII, Seite 75 ff. Ziffer 144–47, 168, 172, 186/187) und fügt erklärend hinzu:

> Mit anderen Worten: Er [Nietzsche] verwirft jede Ethik. Und will nur eine Aesthetik kennen. Der Mensch soll nicht gut, er soll nur ganz sein. Ganz er selbst. Dann ist er schön.
>
> Es leuchtet nebenbei aus seinem Werk als die Hauptsache heraus. Daß das *Starke* für ihn das *Schönste* ist. Es ist eine überraschende Entdeckung. Der Don Juan der ersten Szene des zweiten Teils wäre Nietzsche als der schönste Mensch erschienen.

All das ist sehr sympathisch und steht hoch über all dem ethischen Gefasel von Tausend und Abertausenden. Es ist jedenfalls sehr viel schönheitstrunken zu sein wie er. Ohne Maaß.

Denn er ist schönheitstrunken ohne Maaß. Das Höchste erscheint mir in diesem Augenblick. Ein Schönheitsmaaßbewußtsein. Tasso, Iphigenie. Du siehst wieder den Wertunterschied.

Für die Menschheit Nietzsche.

Für den Menschen Goethe.

Ganz im Sinne Nietzsches überlegt er die ethische Vieldeutigkeit des Wortes:

> Wir können eine Ethik nicht haben—einfach weil etwas, durch ein *Wort ausgedrückt*, immer vieldeutig bleibt und ein ethisches System doch immer in Worten bestehen wird. Für jedes Individuum andersdeutig. Z. B. sage ich: das war grausam so empfindet der schwache Mensch einen Schmerz, Ekel, der starke eine Lust, Freude.
>
> Das Wort "grausam" hat eben keinen feststehenden Wert für alle Menschen und alle Zeiten. Ebenso "selbstlos." Ein Starker nennt es "schlapp" usw. (VII, 848)

Uns scheint diese eingehende Auslegung der Ethik Nietzsches außerordentlich wichtig. Zunächst belegt sie mit ziemlicher Sicherheit die Tatsache, die Paulsen und Wendler bestreiten, daß sich Sternheim zu irgendeiner Zeit einigermaßen intensiv mit Nietzsches Werk selbst beschäftigt hat. Eben hier bezieht sich Sternheim direkt auf das Werk ("es leuchtet nebenbei aus seinem Werk"), hier zitiert er aus dem Werk. Auch handelt es sich kaum um eine flüchtige Bekanntschaft, wobei Nietzsche etwa als Kuriosum oberflächlich durchblättert wird, denn diese Aussage Sternheims kommt zu einer Zeit, wo er sich ja anhaltend mit Philosophie und Ethik beschäftigt hat, wie die Briefe bezeugen. Ferner ist die Aussage gewissermaßen Wiederholung und Bestätigung des zehn Monate früher geschriebenen "Herrenmoral"-Briefes vom Februar 1906.[23]

---

[23] Wie der Nietzsche-Brief vom November 1906 und der "Herrenmoral"-Brief vom 6. Februar 1906 zu einander stehen, ist schwer zu sagen. Man hätte eher die umgekehrte Reihenfolge der Briefe erwartet. Denn die allgemeinen Überlegungen hätten doch der praktischen Übertragung vorangehen sollen. Dies mag denn auch der eigentliche Hergang gewesen sein. Die Beschäftigung mit Nietzsche könnte schon in Rom angefangen haben— in einem anfangs 1905 aus Rom geschriebenen Brief bezieht sich Sternheim auf den Stil Nietzsches hinsichtlich des Stils in Don Juan: "O ihr Thoren, die ihr, wenn ihr knappe dramatische Verse lehrt, meint, der Autor könne nicht sprechen wie Nietzsche, Hofmannsthal. Im Gegenteil . . . Ich meine im Juan die dramatische Sprache Shakespeares oft

Die Intensität und Aufrichtigkeit dieser ethischen Beschäftigung läßt sich besonders daran erkennen, daß er an dem Studium der Philosophie "unendliche Freude" empfindet, obwohl er eingestehen muß, daß es ihm schwer fällt. Auch daran, daß er in dieser Zeit nicht einfach rezeptiv die Meinungen anderer aufnahm, sondern selbst im Gegensatz zum Gehörten und Gelesenen nach einer ethischen Haltung suchte, die Pflicht mit persönlichem Entschluß und Selbstwollen verband. Erst mit der fröhlichen Begrüßung der Moral Nietzsches löste sich für ihn das Problem.

Wie sehr sich Sternheim mit der Nietzsche-Lektüre im besonderen abgab, kann man daran erkennen, daß er die Begriffe verständig und sachlich erfaßt. Hier distanziert sich Sternheim nicht, fügt keine eigenen Meinungen hinzu. Seine Formulierung, "Der Mensch soll nicht gut, er soll nur ganz sein," trifft schon das Wesentliche. Auch übersieht Sternheim das dionysische Moment nicht, auch nicht das Fehlen jeglichen äußeren Maßstabs ("ohne Maaß").[24]

Und nun die positive Stellungnahme zu Nietzsche. Sternheim findet Nietzsches Vorliebe für das Starke "überraschend" und "sehr sympathisch." Was der Immoralist behauptet "steht hoch über all dem ethischen Gefasel von Tausend und Abertausenden." Eine fast unbewußt bejahende Annahme der Nietzscheschen Denkart ist in den Bemerkungen über die ethische Vieldeutigkeit des Wortes zu erkennen.

Wenn man nun zu all dem noch die zeitliche Übereinstimmung der Entdeckung des Kraftbegriffs bei Nietzsche durch Sternheim und das plötzliche Auftauchen dieses Begriffs als Kerngedanke des *Don Juan* nimmt, so kann man nicht umhin, den Schluß zu ziehen: aus dieser Zeit des ethischen Ringens und besonders aus der intensiven Beschäftigung mit der Moral Nietzsches erhielt Sternheim eine entscheidende Anregung, Bestätigung, Klärung seiner eigenen Gedanken. Wir wissen, eben zu diesem Zeitpunkt festigte sich seine ethische Einstellung. Bis dahin unsicher und

---

erreicht zu haben" (VI, 472). In diesem Fall hätte Sternheim früher Durchdachtes, etwa aus einem Tagebuch, seinem späteren, im November geschriebenen Brief eingefügt. Auch so ist aber von Bedeutung, daß er noch zu der früheren Aussage steht.

[24] Damit soll nicht gesagt werden, daß er die Metaphysik Nietzsches begriff. Dafür hatte der in dieser Hinsicht wissenschaftlich orientierte Sternheim wenig Verständnis. An seiner Intelligenz darf aber nicht gezweifelt werden. Obwohl er wie Georg Kaiser, um Sensation zu erregen, nicht ungern große Worte um Dinge machte, die er nicht verstand, so hat Kasimir Edschmid, der ihn gut kannte und sich gelegentlich von Sternheims Meinungen distanzierte, wohl recht in seiner Feststellung: "Er war ein Kindskopf, aber vielleicht der intelligenteste, den ich kannte" (*Lebendiger Expressionismus* [Wien, 1961], S. 129).

konfus, lagert sie sich nun eindeutig um den Kraftbegriff, der lange Jahre die zentrale Stelle einnimmt.[25] Also in dieser Zeit des belegten Nietzsche-Studiums und des belegten weltanschaulichen Umschwungs findet wohl die entscheidende Begegnung mit Nietzsche, die Zeit der Nietzsche-"Beeinflussung" statt.

Übrigens liegt bei Sternheims Begriff der Kraft, der zu dieser Zeit noch recht undifferenziert ist, das Hauptgewicht auf der Stärke, der Vitalität. Don Juan ist in seiner jugendlichen Lebensfülle dem König überlegen. Wenn auch die Kluft Adel—Bürger, Romantik—Biedermeier, die beiden trennt, so stehen in ihrer Verkörperung der Kraft Don Juan und Theobald Maske einander nahe. Wenn einige Jahre später Sternheim Scarrons Geniemoral verwirft, so ist das wohl so zu verstehen, daß Sternheim im Gegensatz zu der immer gängiger werdenden Deutung der Ethik Nietzsches als Geniemoral, an seiner einmal gefaßten Anschauung festhalten wollte. Welche Ironie, daß Sternheim dann nach dem Krieg seinen Kraftbegriff in ein "Beharren bei sich selbst," also doch noch in eine geistige Macht umwandelte!

1905 war Sternheim 27 Jahre alt. Schon vor der Jahrhundertwende studierte er Literaturgeschichte und Philosophie an drei deutschen Universitäten. Da Nietzsche gerade in diesen Jahren Berühmtheit erlangte, ist anzunehmen, daß Sternheim auch vor 1905 mit Nietzsches Ideen bekannt gewesen sein muß.

In den dem *Don Juan* unmittelbar vorangehenden Werken ist jedoch nichts von Nietzsche zu verspüren. Das Hauptwerk des Jahres 1904, *Ulrich und Brigitte* (erst 1907 veröffentlicht), stellt eine romantische Geschwister-Tragödie dar. In den drei Lustspielen des *Abenteuerers*, etwa um dieselbe Zeit konzipiert, ist Casanova zwar der Held, wird aber nur als witziger Lüstling und Till Eulenspiegel aufgefaßt.

Bei den allerfrühesten Versuchen (1895–1900) findet man dann wieder eine Vorliebe zum vorurteilslosen, starken Helden. So siegt Barry in dem etwa 1895 entstandenen Stück *Im Hafen* über den intrigierenden Marquis, da er, obwohl ein leichtlebiger Galan, sich jedoch mutig zu sich selbst bekennt:

---

[25] Die Bedeutung dieses Wandels ist auch Wilhelm Emrich nicht entgangen: "In der Ablösung des Zentralbegriffs der 'Sehnsucht' durch den der 'Kraft,' so undeutlich sie auch noch ist, kündigt sich auch die Konzeption an, die den Komödien zugrunde liegt" (VII, 850–51).

Ich thue, was mir mein Gefühl
Vorschreibt, und halte das für gut und recht.
Der strengen Sitte hündisch feiger Knecht
Mag der sein, der in sich die Kraft nicht fühlt,
EigenenWeg zu gehen, ich spür' den Mut
In mir. (VIII, 17)

In dem Prosafragment *Geschichte eines bedeutenden Mannes* (1898) trägt der
Held deutliche Züge des Herrenmenschen:

> Auch war schon der Augenblick da ich ihn kennen lernte sehr verschieden
> von dem ersten Begegnen mit andern Menschen . . . Woher hatte er auch
> all diese äußern Attribute einer starken Herrschaft? (IX, 590. Gestrichene
> Stellen). Wie schön war dieser Glaube, der tief von sich überzeugt war
> (IX, 325). Wie er frei und groß ging und stand, hierhin und dorthin
> plauderte und überall gehört wurde. . . . (IX, 326)

Die Problematik des starken mitleidslosen Menschen wird in dem
Einakter *Glaube* (etwa 1895) angerührt. Öfter taucht auch im Frühwerk die
Gestalt des Künstlers auf, dem innerer Drang den eigenen Weg zu gehen
vorschreibt.

Ein Gedicht des Jahres 1897 beginnt mit den Zeilen "Originell, um
jeden Preis, sei die Losung" (IX, 24). Bald aber entpuppt sich der Sprecher
als Dandy, dem es nur darum geht: "Im Sein und im Handeln anders als
andere." "Freiheit der Meinung" wird "Respektlosigkeit" gleichgesetzt.

In der von Stefan George stilistisch stark beeinflußten Gedichtsamm-
lung *Fanale* (1901) finden sich Hinweise auf den genialen, stark erlebenden
Künstler. Im Vorwort heißt es: "Mag einem, dem Natur das Talent in die
Wiege gab, auch die Möglichkeit nicht genommen sein, in starkem
Erleben die angestammte Herrlichkeit zu genialer Größe zu vervollkomm-
nen" (VII, 8). Und in dem Gedicht "Strahlendes Erkennen":

> Wenn kleines Menschentum ich um mich merke . . .
> Man muß ganz strahlend aus sich selber leuchten. (VII, 17)

Die meisten Gedichte dieser Sammlung sind jedoch mit jugendlicher
Erotik so sehr befrachtet, daß man unwillkürlich an Sternheims wohl
ironisch gemeinte Zeilen von 1897 denken muß:

Wenn ich nur nicht immer schriebe
Meine schlüpfrig seichten Verse
Meine höchst perverse Lyrik. (IX, 28)

Nietzsche wird auch in einem Gedicht aus dieser Zeit erwähnt (1901):

Ich glaube Nietzsche auch, trotz Jesu Christ,
Ich glaube auch, daß Irren menschlich ist,
Ich glaub' an Raffael und Mozart, Goethen,
Und trotzdem ist ein Glaube mir von nöthen. (IX, 86)

Es handelt sich hier offensichtlich um die Ethik Nietzsches, die mit den christlichen Glaubensgeboten verglichen wird. Der leichte Ton verrät aber, wie wenig ernst es Sternheim dabei war, wie wenig er sich noch um ethische Dinge kümmerte.

Aus den veröffentlichten Werken der Frühzeit läßt sich also keine tiefere Beschäftigung Sternheims mit Nietzsche feststellen. Es mag vielleicht in den unveröffentlichten Heften des in Marbach befindlichen Sternheim-Archivs noch dieser oder jener frühe Bezug zu Nietzsche zu entdecken sein. Es ist aber kaum anzunehmen, daß sie den Tatbestand wesentlich ändern würden.

★   ★   ★

Fassen wir zusammen: Schon das Frühwerk Sternheims weist selbstsichere, vorurteilslose Menschen auf, und die Frage nach der ethischen Sonderstellung des starken Menschen und des Künstlers wird gelegentlich angerührt. 1901 legt Sternheim ein leichtfertiges Glaubensbekenntnis zu Nietzsche ab. Es ist aus all dem anzunehmen, daß er in diesen frühen Jahren in der Schule über Nietzsche gehört, vielleicht den *Zarathustra* gelesen, und von an Nietzsche orientierten Schriftstellern wie Stefan George diesbezügliche Eindrücke erhalten hat. Von einem näheren Verhältnis zu Nietzsche kann aber noch nicht die Rede sein.

Bei der 1905 in Angriff genommenen Arbeit an *Don Juan* kommen Sternheim Bedenken hinsichtlich der ethischen Erfassung seines Helden. Da das Stück ihm besonders nahe geht, wird die eigene Weltanschauung miteinbezogen. Am Anfang des Jahres 1906 vertieft er sich plötzlich in ethische Studien, die er im Zusammenhang mit Vorlesungsbesuchen in

Freiburg im Laufe des Jahres fortsetzt. Gegen die hergebrachte Schulphilo-sophie versucht er seine eigene Meinung zu formulieren, kommt aber zunächst nicht recht vom Fleck. Erst bei der jubelnden Besprechung der Ethik Nietzsches, die als vom Begriff der Stärke ausgehend aufgefaßt wird, lösen sich die ethischen Schwierigkeiten. Wie sehr Sternheim dieser subjek-tiven Ethik der Stärke verfallen ist, wird an dem drastischen Umschwung in der Gestaltung des Don Juan deutlich. Seine neue Haltung wird auch in dem Stück *Die Hose* und den damit verwandten Komödien ersichtlich.

In der Komödie *Die Hose*, durch die Sternheim berühmt wurde, ist die Auseinandersetzung mit Nietzsche der wesentliche gedankliche Inhalt. Sternheim distanziert sich hier zwar vom geistigen Geniemenschen, hält aber im Grunde an dem von Nietzsche übernommenen, bzw. angeregten Kraftbegriff fest. Nach dem ersten Weltkrieg setzt sich Sternheim in dem Roman *Europa* wiederum eingehend mit Nietzsche auseinander. "Wille zur Macht" als Ursache brutaler Kriege und kultureller Selbstvernichtung wird nun abgelehnt. Der Kraftbegriff wird aber als der "Trieb reinen Lebens" beibehalten. In dem *Berlin*-Aufsatz spricht Sternheim dann auch von der maßgeblichen Bedeutung der "Kraft der Vision." Von her-kömmlicher Ethik will er aber noch nichts wissen. Wie immer soll der Mensch lebensbejahend auf sich selbst hören und nach wie vor bleibt die Stärke des inneren Erlebens das entscheidende Kriterium. Wiederholt wird in sehr positivem Sinne auf Nietzsche gewiesen. In den *Juste-Milieu*-Schriften dieser Jahre wird er sogar als der einzige, der Europa hätte retten können, dargestellt, wenn ihm auch Sternheim seine eigene Adaption der Nietzschelehre unterschiebt. Erst in den allerletzten Jahren seiner literari-schen Tätigkeit (1936), zu einer Zeit also, da man den Namen Nietzsches vielfach in Verbindung mit dem Nationalsozialismus brachte, lehnte Sternheim Nietzsche samt seiner Lehre ab, wie es auch viele andere deutsche Schriftsteller, die in einem engeren Verhältnis zu Nietzsche standen, wie z. B. Thomas Mann, Hermann Hesse, Robert Musil, taten.

Was man auch von Sternheims bizarrer Weltanschauung halten mag— seine brutale Ironie und übertriebene Erotik erregen heute noch heftigen Anstoß—, er war ein ursprünglicher und konsequent denkender Mann. Mit Recht kann aber gesagt werden, daß er sich fast zwei Jahrzehnte immer wieder, und mehr als mit irgendeinem anderen, mit Nietzsche auseinander-gesetzt hat. Ohne die immer wiederkehrende Bezugnahme auf die Moral Nietzsches hätte das Hauptwerk Sternheims wohl ein ganz anderes Gesicht erhalten.

Nietzsche and Georg Kaiser

The history of research dealing with the impact of Nietzsche on Georg Kaiser spans over three decades and is a record of erratic progress toward a goal that has not yet been reached. In 1926, when the dramatist was still at the height of his fame and little was known about his personal life and views, Max Freyhan discussed briefly Nietzschean aspects in two of Kaiser's plays, *Der gerettete Alkibiades* and *Gats*[1]; two years later Hugo F. Koenigsgarten boldly declared that Kaiser was a disciple of Nietzsche by virtue of his strong and recurrent plea for the vitalistic regeneration of man.[2] Koenigsgarten stated his view summarily without documentation but with such clarity and force that scholars must certainly have cocked their ears and considered the possibility of a detailed investigation of the relationship. However, after the pacifistic playwright was blacklisted by the Nazis in 1933, critical writing on him virtually ceased until the end of hostilities and Kaiser's death in 1945. In the late forties and early fifties a number of doctoral candidates[3] had the opportunity to peruse various portions of the literary remains, now housed for the most part in the Kaiser archive in the Akademie der Künste in Berlin, and although they were not primarily interested in the subject under consideration, jointly accumulated evidence indicating that Kaiser had indeed concerned himself with Nietzsche. The main facts can be listed briefly.

The dramatist first became acquainted with the ideas of Nietzsche in a lecture by Kurt Hildebrandt, later to become a renowned Nietzsche scholar, held in the literary club, Sappho (co-founded by Kaiser and Hans Hildebrandt around 1895). *Also sprach Zarathustra* was the first work to

---

[1] Max Freyhan, *Georg Kaisers Werk* (Berlin, 1926), pp. 337, 364.

[2] Hugo F. Koenigsgarten, *Georg Kaiser* (Potsdam, 1928), pp. 68, 70.

[3] Most important are Viktor Fürdauer, *Georg Kaisers dramatisches Gesamtwerk* (Diss. Vienna, 1949); Wolfgang Fix, *Die Ironie im Drama Georg Kaisers* (Diss. Heidelberg, 1951); Hanns H. Fritze, *Über das Problem der Zivilisation im Schaffen Georg Kaisers* (Diss. Freiburg, 1953).

awaken Kaiser's strong enthusiasm. While in Argentina, he read avidly in the works of Dostoevsky, Schopenhauer and Nietzsche; and upon his return to Germany he held long conversations on the philosopher with an old Sappho-friend, Wilhelm Andreae. In 1904, Kaiser conceived plans for a drama dealing with the superman and jotted down notes and extracts from Nietzsche's writings. The following year he entered for a short time into relations with Kurt Hildebrandt and other members of the Nietzsche-oriented George circle. In 1919, he wrote a drama which he said contained all of Nietzsche and Plato, and in 1938 outlined a Nietzsche play that was to be entitled *Ariadne*.[4]

One would think that, as this information became known, it would have occasioned a new effort to ascertain Kaiser's exact debt to Nietzsche, but scholars were evidently unwilling to perform the task. Several reasons for this lack of interest can, of course, easily be deduced. For one thing, the notion was widely held that Plato had exerted a stronger influence on Kaiser than Nietzsche. Then, after the war, many German scholars vigorously rejected what they considered to be the dangerous subjectivism of Nietzsche's doctrine. Lastly, this was only one problem in the vast backlog of problems in the field of German literature that had accumulated during the war.

In any case, little was done. Hanns H. Fritze,[5] Hansres Jacobi[6] and others touched on the subject of Nietzsche's influence, but that was all. B. J. Kenworthy, in his comprehensive English study (1958), contented himself with a few references and the comment that Kaiser owed to Plato, Nietzsche and Christ "a particular debt . . . which is apparent in so much of his work."[7]

Wolfgang Paulsen deliberated on the matter at some length in his Kaiser monograph (1960), but then came to the conclusion that Nietzsche had not significantly shaped Kaiser's outlook.[8]

Paulsen was willing to admit that all of Kaiser's thought rested in the shadow of the early and decisive Nietzsche experience:

---

[4] Ariadne, as the beloved of Dionysus, had especial significance for Nietzsche.

[5] Fritze, p. 83.

[6] Hansres Jacobi, *Amphitryon in Frankreich und Deutschland* (Zurich, 1952), p. 111.

[7] B. J. Kenworthy, *Georg Kaiser* (Oxford, 1957), p. 42.

[8] Wolfgang Paulsen, *Georg Kaiser: Die Perspektiven seines Werkes* (Tübingen, 1960). Plays by Kaiser mentioned in this study are dated in accordance with Paulsen's bibliography.

Unser Bild wäre ohne den erneuten Hinweis auf Nietzsche nicht vollstän-dig, nicht einmal richtig, denn was Kaiser sich auch im Verlauf seines Lebens geistig angeeignet hat, es wurde immer wieder durch dieses frühe und bestimmende Erlebnis gefiltert und gewandelt.[9]

However, this critic was reluctant to believe that the encounter with Nietzsche had been more than an emotional experience for Kaiser[10]; not ideas but the "Eindruck der großen pathetischen Geste" was what Kaiser had gained from his nineteenth-century predecessor.[11] In Paulsen's opinion the dramatist had never read Nietzsche with care, excluding the latter's criticism of Socrates, and like many of his contemporaries had absorbed Nietzschean ideas from the *Zeitgeist* by a kind of osmosis.[12] Nor did Kaiser's early plays get very close to the heart of Nietzsche's ideology, according to Paulsen, since the "blond beast" was conspicuously absent in a milieu where he might have committed all kinds of mischief,[13] and so Paulsen concluded: "es kann doch auch keine Frage darüber bestehen, daß für Kaiser dies alles zunächst eine recht literarische Angelegenheit blieb."[14]

From the foregoing two things should now be clear: that there is no agreement as yet in the critical literature on the subject of Nietzsche's influence on Kaiser, and that no comprehensive discussion of the problem has been undertaken. Although the limits of this paper do not permit an exhaustive analysis, it will endeavor to present an objective evaluation of the extent and manner of Nietzsche's influence on Georg Kaiser.

As a point of departure for our inquiry, *Der gerettete Alkibiades* seems particularly well suited, since it was over a decade in the making,[15] and since it was with respect to this comedy that the playwright had once written that it contained all of Plato and all of Nietzsche, and that it

---

[9] *Ibid.*, p. 103. Paulsen also says that the Nietzsche influence "gilt auch für die grie-chischen Dramen" (p. 105).

[10] *Ibid.*, p. 104.

[11] *Ibid.*, p. 113. The pathos in Kaiser's plays (pp. 103–104) as well as the arrogant and prophetic tone of his essays and final aphorisms (p. 106) also reflected Nietzsche's influence.

[12] *Ibid.*, p. 104.

[13] *Ibid.*, p. 17.

[14] *Ibid.*, pp. 16–17.

[15] It will be shown that Kaiser had the motif in mind since 1904. See also Bernhard Diebold, *Der Denkspieler Georg Kaiser* (Frankfurt am Main, 1924), p. 20: "Nur am *Geretteten Alkibiades* soll er zehn Jahre lang gefeilt haben."

destroyed the classic conception of antiquity (implying to a large degree acceptance of Nietzsche's dionysiac doctrine):

Der ganze Platon [ist] darin—der ganze Nietzsche—und alles aufgelöst in szenischer blutvollster Gestaltung. Ich habe Griechenland neu geschaffen— und das des Goethe, Winckelmann umgestürzt. Die Menschheit muß mir danken—oder es gibt sie nicht. . . .[16]

Nietzsche's influence is first apparent in the manner in which the Athenians in the play view Socrates, regarding him as the embodiment of mind maliciously opposed to life. For them he is not Plato's gadfly stinging the great steed of Athens into wakeful vitality, but rather a cunning dialectical thinker opposed to instinct—the Socrates portrayed by Nietzsche in *Geburt der Tragödie* and other writings.

This Athenian concept of Socrates is repeatedly highlighted throughout the play. It was because of his idealistic teachings that the youth of Athens determined to renounce life, as symbolized in their rejection of gymnastics and sports. As a result of his dialectical harangues, he completely confused the natural, instinctive actions of the litter-bearers and fishmongers. Only because Alcibiades was convinced that Socrates posed a mortal danger to life, did the young general topple the great hermae on the market square.

Obviously such parallelism was not the product of mere chance. That Kaiser had, indeed, the Nietzschean conception of Socrates clearly in mind when he wrote the play is evident from a jotting attached to the manuscript in the *Nachlaß*:

SOKRATES (RICHARD III)

Mit seinem Tode, weil er das Leben mißachtet(?) feiert er den größten Triumph.—Faßte man Christus nicht ebenso auf: der Machtlose, der nach der Macht begehrt? Sokrates aus Tücke—Christus aus Mitleid? . . . — Instinktiv wird Sokrates von den Athenern verurteilt—quod juventutem corrumpsit!—Bin ich gewillt ein Bösewicht zu werden: das absichtsvolle Steigern seines Verlustes. Saure Trauben! Aus der Not die Tugend.[17]

As early as 1904, when he had written down extracts from Nietzsche's

---

[16] Alfred Beierle, "Begegnung mit Georg Kaiser," *Aufbau*, 2 (Berlin, 1948), 990.
[17] Fix, p. 168.

"Problem des Sokrates," in which the sage is viewed as a deceptive clown,[18] the playwright had envisioned a drama comparing the death of the *Übermensch* with that of the *Vernunftmensch* and wrote several comments in this connection. The last of these reads: "Ich komme auf Nietzsche—Wahrheit und Macht."[19] One may fairly presume that as the antithesis of the superman he had Socrates in mind, conceived as a sophistic dialectician striving for power.

What now of the Socrates whom the audience sees? He is just the opposite of what the Athenians think he is, since not one of his dramatically heroic acts is motivated either by conventional idealism or malice. He invents the myth of idealism out of sympathy for Alcibiades, regrets the unfortunate turn of events caused by this invention, exhorts Xantippe to defend life, and dies because he apparently cannot bear to witness the coming trumph of idealism. For the audience, Socrates is a clear-cut exponent of vitalism. In his final moments, Socrates himself mourned the fact that his idealism had dealt vitalism a mortal blow—in the manner conceived by Nietzsche:

> . . . einmal müssen sich die andern auflehnen und einen Himmel über den Himmel türmen, aus dem die Sonne so furchtbar brennt, wie sie es schwächlich nicht ertragen!—mich schmerzte der Wandel—und es verurteilte mich zur Standhaftigkeit! (I, 108)[20]

Since vitalism is a Nietzschean tenet which in modern times has helped to topple classical idealism in Germany, and since Socrates has been shown to contain within himself the usual Kaiser dichotomy of *Geist* versus *Leben*, which satisfies the structural requirements of the drama, this might appear the proper point to conclude the interpretation. However, one basic question remains unanswered: why does Socrates renounce for himself the joys of life when he is an exponent of life? One thinks immediately of the thorn. But it is precisely because of the thorn, as will be shown below, that he should have wanted to partake of life. We suggest that a dialectical

---

[18] *Ibid.*, pp. 40–41.

[19] *Ibid.*, pp. 40–41.

[20] Although this Nietzsche-Kaiser article first appeared before the publication of Georg Kaiser's complete works, all references are to this edition: *Werke*, ed. Walther Huder, 6 vols. (Frankfurt am Main: Propyläen Verlag, 1970–1972). Volume and page number will be given in the body of the text.

confrontation of optimistic vitalism with pessimistic vitalism may have been Kaiser's deepest layer of meaning.

The nucleus of this hypothesis is the all-important thorn. Freyhan was wrong in believing the thorn to be merely the incipient of the action, since it is also the symbol of the play's ultimate meaning. Kaiser said as much when he wrote: "Mächtig schafft Mythos im Sinnbild—und im kleinsten Ding des Splitters eines Dorns—beweist er seine schöpferische Macht."[21] All of Kaiser's activating objects have symbolic value as well. To give only a few examples: Nehrkorn's mousetrap stands for his vain attempt to ensnare life, the billionaire's coral represents the security of an island retreat, the gas of the latter's progeny depicts the destructive force of mechanized civilization, and Krehler's papiermâché globe symbolizes his futile yearning for life.

What is the thorn? It is the sharp prod of instinct. In two other plays, *Die jüdische Witwe* (1904–1908; I, 167) and *Gilles und Jeanne* (1922),[22] the one written before and the other after the completion of *Der gerettete Alkibiades*, a thorn also represents instinct. In these other plays, however, the thorn pricks a virile representative of life and symbolizes frustrated sexual longing. In the case of Socrates the situation is different, as the thorn is brought into contact with mind and causes a unique pain that induces him to renounce life.[23] Such pain can only result from the confrontation of instinct with mind; if instinct alone were the cause, what would be the logic of having the pain induce Socrates to resist the lure of the attractive concubine and shun fame? Why would it make him, even before the trial, see in death a welcome release from "Lob—Leiden—Leben?" Or, to put the problem differently, would not Alcibiades, who was hailed into court by his wife for adultery, suffer far more than Socrates? In this play only Socrates has a thorn; it has virtually become a part of him. Thus it is clear that the true symbol of the drama is the limping Socrates—which is the picture that the play-goer carries away with him.

[21] Koenigsgarten, p. 9.

[22] *Gilles und Jeanne* (V, 782). After Jeanne's death the alchemist says to Gilles: "Jetzt bist du—frei. Der Stachel ist aus dem Fleisch gebrannt" (V, 773).

[23] The thorn is employed as a symbol of life's troubles in *Adrienne Ambrossat*: "Wir sind in diesem Dornstrauch verfangen und finden keinen Ausweg" (III, 332). And in *Gas II* the hero says, "Front dem Fremden . . . verleugnet den Stachel, der an euch blutet:—seid das Reich" (II, 86). In *Die Koralle* broken pieces of coral have the same function: "Losgebrochene Stücke vom dämmernden Korallenbaum—mit einer Wunde vom ersten Tag an. Die schließt sich nicht—die brennt uns—unser fürchterlicher Schmerz hetzt uns die Laufbahn!" (I, 711).

What does the limping Socrates represent? In a word, the depressing corollary which the new revelation of the primacy of instinct brings to his keen mind: the knowledge that man is earthbound, a creature of the flesh, and that all ideals are illusory. Such an attitude explains fully Socrates' renunciation of life. He welcomes death not to enter a spirit world—there is none; not to deceive Plato into believing he is an idealist; but as a vitalist aware of the pain of life, the fraudulency of idealism, the chaos of existence. He dies a nihilist.

But his nihilism is not complete and does not rule out love of life in the sense of love for one's fellow men. In his last words to Xantippe, Socrates had described love as "das ungewiß gewisseste von allen Wundern" (I, 808), a miracle that chance kept alive in an otherwise chaotic and meaningless world. Love for his fellows had induced the aged thinker to hide the secret of nihilism from them, and to give his life rather than reveal the horrible secret—"es kostet ein Leben das zu ersticken" (I, 812).

Socrates overcame dionysiac reality by synthesizing idealism and nihilism, by detecting the possibility of a new idealism within the framework of nihilism, but his optimism is of the order of Thomas Mann's wan hope in the final pages of *Dr. Faustus* that a miracle may come to pass; Socrates affirms and overcomes nihilism in the tragic sense of *amor fati*.

Some years ago it was fashionable to consider Kaiser as a *Denkspieler* whose heart was never in his work. Scholars now know that the dramatist was personally and deeply involved in his art, and that many of his heroes spoke for him. Socrates was one of his favorites with whom he identified himself most closely. Not only do we know that he concerned himself with the sage since 1904, but in 1929 when he planned to write a book castigating the follies of the times, he made Socrates his spokesman. *Ächtung des Kriegers*, the one extant chapter of *Sokrates wandelnd heute*, makes the identification abundantly clear. Again, years later while in exile, Kaiser identified himself in bitter jest with Socrates, commenting in a letter to a friend that he, too, was fattening the fowl with which to welcome death: "Ich bin längst dem Tode näher als dem Leben. Und schon mäste ich den Hahn, den ich nach sokratischer Art opfern werde, wenn ich das hinter mir habe, was sich Leben nennt."[24] It is evident that a nihilistic Socrates would have most accurately represented Kaiser's deep sense of disillusionment in the post-war years, as expressed in the *Gas* trilogy and in the bitter comments he made during his trial in 1921.

---

[24] T. Risti [Robert Pirk], "Georg Kaisers dramatische Sendung," *Schweizer Annalen*, 2 (1945), 544.

Further support for this interpretation of Socrates may be seen in the fact that Kaiser incorporated elements into the play borrowed from a Nietzschean aphorism in which Socrates is clearly conceived as a nihilist. There is an unmistakable verbal parallelism between Kaiser's death scene and that in aphorism 340 in *Die fröhliche Wissenschaft*, in which Nietzsche had imbued Socrates with his own pessimism and had interpreted the latter's words, "Oh Kriton, ich bin dem Asklepios einen Hahn schuldig," to mean that life was tragic and death beneficial. To cite Nietzsche's words: "Dieses lächerliche und furchtbare 'letzte Wort' heißt für Den [sic], der Ohren hat! 'Oh Kriton, *das Leben ist eine Krankheit!*' " It has already been shown that the young Plato in Kaiser's play interpreted Socrates' last words similarly, using the same key-word, *Krankheit*: "So schied Socrates vom Leben, wie von einer langen Krankheit—und dankte dem Tode wie einem Arzt, der ihn von schwerem Leiden erlöst!" (I, 813). Nietzsche had continued:

> Ist es möglich! Ein Mann wie er, der heiter und vor aller Augen wie ein Soldat gelebt hat—war Pessimist! Er hatte eben nur eine gute Miene zum Leben gemacht und zeitlebens sein letztes Urtheil, sein innerstes Gefühl versteckt! Sokrates, Sokrates hat *am Leben gelitten!*

In Nietzsche's eyes, Socrates had been a pessimist throughout his life.

Of course, it may be argued that Kaiser may well have used the words without necessarily retaining the meaning of the aphorism. This possibility seems unlikely, however, when one recalls that the aging Kaiser used the identical figure of speech to express his intense dissatisfaction with life.

Still another factor lends weight to the hypothesis of nihilism: the extent to which Kaiser's drama parallels *Also sprach Zarathustra*. In the one as in the other, a sage comes upon a dreadful secret concerning the nature of being which is so terrible that he feels compelled to hide it from his fellow men. In each case the secret has to do with the nihilistically conceived universe that lies under the façade of idealism. In each case the hero seeks to isolate himself. In each case, at the moment of death, by reference to a miraculous event, life is reaffirmed within the framework of nihilism; Zarathustra grasped at the notion of the eternal recurrence whereas Socrates hoped for a miracle after the manner of love. To be sure, Nietzsche's sage lives on and Socrates seeks death, but the difference is slight; actually Socrates has a glimmer of hope, whereas Zarathustra despite his affirmation continues to view life as infinitely tragic.

The close identification of Kaiser's Socrates with Zarathustra fails only with respect to the new ideal they extoll. It is clear that Socrates personified love and that his outlook included elements of Platonic or Christian idealism as well as the Nietzschean doctrine of a soulless universe. However, it will be shown that this paradoxical union did not disturb the roots of Kaiser's Nietzschean premises.

There is clearly much to speak for the third interpretation of Socrates as a tragic vitalist, but whether one prefer the second or the third interpretation, whether one prefer the conventional superman or Zarathustra, optimistic or pessimistic vitalism, both derive from Nietzsche and his contribution to the play is evident.

Now, to see whether Kaiser merely used Nietzschean concepts as a chance occurrence, or whether they reflected an attitude of long-standing, we may now proceed to the early plays and have chosen as the one best suited for our purposes, *Rektor Kleist* (1905), rather than the thematically similar *Der Schüler Vegesack* (1901–02),[25] as the former brings certain Nietzschean aspects into clearer focus. Granted, no trace of a "blond beast" can be found, but neither was there a ruthless superman in the Nietzschean play just discussed. Conversely, one discovers in *Rektor Kleist* a very similar set of antagonists. A gymnastics instructor named Kornmüller has, like Alcibiades, all the attributes of the biological superman. Kornmüller enjoys excellent health and his virility is attested to by his strong and healthy children. He prides himself on his "gesunden Instinkte," and is "heilfroh, daß es in mir noch zu brausen vermag" (V, 236). But Kornmüller, again like the Greek general, has only average intelligence and holds determinedly and at times rather blindly to conventional notions of morality and truth— the earthy name Kornmüller has also a petty-bourgeois ring.

His opponent is Rektor Kleist, a sickly little hunchback approaching middle age. A light beard hints at impotence; foppish dress at a desire to be accepted: "Er ist ein kleiner, schmächtiger Mann . . . geckenhaft gekleidet. Wenig über fünfzig Jahre alt. Die rechte Schulter ist hoch verwachsen. Dünnes, rötliches mit Grau vermischtes Haar, geringer Backenbart, Brille mit Goldrand" (V, 225). Despite his weakness, or because of it, he craves life strongly, inordinately: "Was locken uns die Traumbilder des Ruhms am meisten? Was machen sie uns schlaflos und vor der Zeit begierig? Weib-Kind-Ruhm, was gilt der Geist vor der Tat?" (V, 271). Courageous-

---

[25] *Der Schüler Vegesack* pits a beardless rector against a healthy young student, with the former getting involved in an incident by going to the student's room.

ly, if foolishly, he prefers to suffer the unspeakable torment of painful hemorrhoids rather than permit their removal—which would entail revealing the nature of his ailment and thereby make him the laughing stock of the community.

Kleist's sickness and thwarted desire make him bitter and resentful toward his more fortunate fellows, the strong and healthy, and occasionally lead him to commit an injustice, as when he refused young Strauss leave to go home. This weakness in turn makes him disgusted with himself: "Ich bin mir selbst zum Ekel" (V, 239). But Kleist is by no means a mere villain or weak coward. He has sensitivity and feeling and in his heart wishes the boys no harm. When he returns from the conference at which young Strauss was found guilty, he is despondent at the injustice committed. When the news comes that little Fehse has killed himself, Kleist is beside himself with grief and torment. Nor is he unkind to his attractive and sensible young wife, Frau Sophie, although frequently irascible because of his extremely painful ailment. It must also be remembered that Kleist was to a large degree justified in trying to keep the ink-throwing episode a secret, as he was fully aware that his future and the future of the school were at stake. All his purported evil acts were attempts to forestall the dangerous revelation which the bumbling self-righteous Kornmüller forced to the fore. He remained silent at the council meeting because of his excessive sensitivity to ridicule and because he realized that if the affair became known, he would never live it down, whereas he was convinced that the minor punishment to be inflicted on the boys would be quickly forgotten by all concerned.

Admittedly, one must proceed with caution in the analysis. Kleist does reach a low point when he hurls the epithet "Kanaille" at the sensitive little hunchback, Fehse, and when he cannot bring himself to confess his guilt before the council. But he has done virtually everything that is *for him* humanly possible. When it seemed that Fehse would not co-operate, Kleist *did* confess to Kornmüller and his confession was sincere. One need only to consider the tone of his words which are not smoothly hypocritical, but which are impulsive and intense. Bitterly he says to Kornmüller, "Ihrem Wahrheitsfanatismus ist das Opfer gebracht: ich bin der Täter." (V, 262). When Kornmüller refuses to believe him, Kleist blurts out, "Ich bekenne mich dazu!" (V, 263). And, in increasing agony of soul, "Herr Kornmüller, so hören Sie doch auf mich!" (V, 263). In frustration, he repeats his assertion and asks whether he must spell it out in black and white: "Ich—ich—ich bin der Urheber—ich, Ihr Rektor Richard Kleist! Soll ich es Ihnen niederschreiben, daß Sie dann glauben?" (V, 263). If necessary, he says, he will even explain how the drawing by Strauss entered into the matter, although he pleads in inner torment, "aber ersparen Sie mir die Demütigung" (V, 263).

In a later scene, when Kornmüller claims to know the culprit and suddenly clasps Kleist's arm, the rector is not taken aback, but says with a note of tragedy in his voice, "Warum erhörten Sie mich nicht, als ich Ihnen am Vormittag die Wahrheit preisgab?" (V, 269).

Inasmuch as Kaiser uses a dialectical procedure even in this early play, it may be argued that Kleist spoke, despite the apparent sincerity of his tone, with tongue in cheek, hoping to throw Kornmüller off the track. The only means that is then left to prove this contention in error, is to seek an objective clue outside the speeches of the two men. Such a clue is to be found in the attitude and conviction of Kleist's wife, who like Xantippe and all the sympathetically drawn female characters in Kaiser's dramas, has an unerring sense of right and wrong far beyond all conventional standards of morality. Frau Sophie—healthy, sensible, alert, fond of Kornmüller and his children, a symbol of life and instinct—after carefully evaluating the situation and at first doubting her husband, ultimately places the entire blame on Kornmüller: "Ja, Sie sind es einzig und allein, der an meinem Mann dies Verbrechen verübt hat!" (V, 273). Kornmüller had been too stupid to recognize that her husband's confession of guilt had been sincere: "Der sie (die Wahrheit) verhöhnte, als sie Ihnen von ihm geboten wurde" (V, 273). Through Frau Sophie the author informs us that the rector had done everything in his power to avert the catastrophe, and is not to be held responsible. In a limited sense Kleist is a tragic hero; one feels that he has the sympathy of Kaiser, the morbid—and at the time still sickly—intellectual.

Of particular significance to our investigation is the fact that Kleist is as free of conventional notions as is the later Socrates. The foregoing discussion makes it quite clear that Kleist is voicing his sincere conviction when he argues, in line with Nietzsche's views, that truth can be a dangerously destructive force:

Was ist Wahrheit?—Die Wahrheit am Ende vernichtet uns alle! Sie ist nicht das rosenrote Gebilde, das Sie sich vorzaubern—oder das Schwert, das ein guter Schild noch auffängt. Die Wahrheit—trachten Sie der nach, Herr Kollege, trachten Sie der blindlings nach; so gelangen Sie mit zerschmettertem Schädel auf dem Grunde an. Gott schütze uns Menschen vor der Wahrheit in jeglichem Dinge! (V, 262)

Kleist stresses the illusory nature of conventional justice and conventional mores:

Irrtum—Irrtum—Irrtum, wir sind Kinder des Irrtums, aus Irrtum gezeugt
—wuchernd im Irrtum—Sie wollen Fackelträger heißen und schwenken
mit wilden Gebärden nur eine riesenhafte schwarze Fahne, mit der Sie das
Licht erst recht verdunkeln. . . . Suchen Sie keinen Feuersäulenruhm,—die
Menge rennt den Irrlichtern nach . . . Aus Priestern werdet Ihr zu Henkern
—Menschenopfer einem unbekannten Gott!—Das Maß eurer Gerechtig-
keit sei euch das Leiden beider Parteien! (V, 270)

The ailing rector bears a resemblance to Kaiser's Socrates, and it is interesting to note that Socrates was in the author's mind when he created Kleist.
Arguing against Kornmüller's contention that the Greeks had developed
the body as much as the mind, Kleist cries: "Der größte Grieche war
Sokrates! Ihr Rektor ist auch kein Riese!" (V, 237). Like Socrates, Kleist
is a hero of the intellect, engaged in a bout with brutish life.

The moral relativism and nihilism apparent in the theme of this drama
link it with *Der gerettete Alkibiades* and with Nietzsche. The best indication
that the play reveals a close familiarity on the part of the author with
Nietzschean concepts lies, however, neither in the theme nor in the emphasis on Kornmüller's *gesunde Instinkte*, but in the character of Kleist himself.

Many critics have rightly noted the influence of Wedekind's *Frühlings
Erwachen* on *Rektor Kleist*, but it is obvious that Kaiser's characters do not
derive from that drama. And a moment's reflection will make it equally
obvious that neither Kleist nor Kornmüller is typical of Wedekind's male
heroes. It is well known that Wedekind stood strongly under Nietzschean
influence and that his male heroes are usually strong, brutal, highly sexed,
cunning, amoral individuals—Gerardo and the Marquis von Keith, to mention only two—who combine rather than separate the elements of *Leben*
and *Geist*. Oddly and perhaps significantly, though to our knowledge
nowhere mentioned by critics, there is one play and only one by Wedekind
which might conceivably have influenced Kaiser's characterisation. *Hidalla*
(1904) is an atypical Wedekind drama, heavy with disillusionment and
irony, which in a crucial scene pits a muscular dullard against a keen and
embittered hunchback. Mocking the idealism he had expounded in *Mine-
Haha*, Wedekind portrayed the greasily handsome Morosini, President of
the Society for the *Züchtung von Rassenmenschen* [!] with such ironical
derision that he might well have served as a partial model for Kornmüller,
particularly since Hetmann, the hunchback, with his physical ugliness, his
fanatical drive, his bitter resentfulness, and his keen intellect might have
served as a prototype for Kleist. On closer inspection, however, it becomes

apparent that there is an intrinsic difference between the two hunchbacks. Hetmann is neither weak nor sickly, and there is no indication that his intellectuality or deformity in any way affect his virility. Had he not insisted on remaining a bachelor in conformity with his fanatical ideal of fostering physical beauty, it seems a foregone conclusion that he would have made a model husband. Thus, Hetmann can only have served at best as a partial prototype for Kleist as he, like other Wedekind heroes, represents *Leben* as well as *Geist*.

In these same years, another writer who admitted deriving his concept of *Leben* from Nietzsche, Thomas Mann, wrote several stories that incorporate the dualism of *Leben* versus *Geist*. In *Tristan* (1902) for example, the decadent artist, Spinell, clearly embodies intellectuality whereas the merchant Klöterjahn, stands for insensitive vitality. The hero in *Tonio Kröger* (1903) feels himself straddling two worlds as he has some of the sentimentality and conventionalism of the healthy burgher as well as the icy intellectuality of the enervated artist, and the two worlds have their explicit representatives in Inge, Hans Hansen, and the Hamburg merchant on the one hand and the sickly but artistic Magdalena Vermehren on the other. But here again, whereas the representatives of *Leben*, particularly Klöterjahn and the Hamburg merchant, resemble Kornmüller and might have influenced his creation, Mann's heroes of the intellect are artists and Kleist is no artist.

Whom now does Kleist resemble? Who was his prototype? To some degree Hetmann and Spinell are possibilities, but even more their direct forebear, Socrates, as customarily conceived by Nietzsche! It will be recalled once again, that for Nietzsche a variant of his favorite dichotomy: strength versus weakness, was instinct versus reason, and that he made a sharp distinction between "instinctive" intelligence and dialectical reasoning, detesting the latter as a sign of decadence and weakness. Thus Nietzsche wrote, "Der Pöbel kam mit der Dialektik zum Sieg,"[26] and "Dialektik kann nur eine Notwehr sein." Again, "Die Ironie des Dialektikers ist eine Form der Pöbelrache." The symbol par excellence of the decadent dialectician for Nietzsche had been, from the beginning, Socrates, whom he bitterly attacked not only in his first major work, *Geburt der Tragödie*, but— with a few notable exceptions—throughout his writings. Here are references to Socrates from the posthumous volume, *Wille zur Macht*:

[26] The following quotations from Nietzsche occur in the *Musarion Edition* of his works (XVIII, 306–308).

die Reaktion des Sokrates, welcher die Dialektik als Weg zur Tugend anempfahl . . . bedeutet exakt die Auflösung der griechischen Instinkte. *Verhäßlichung:* Die Selbstverhöhnung, die dialektische Dürre, die Klugheit als *Tyrann* gegen den "Tyrannen" (den Instinkt). Es ist alles übertrieben [Kaiser uses "geckenhaft"] excentrisch, Caricatur an Sokrates, ein buffo mit den Instinkten Voltaires im Leibe . . . er vertritt nichts als die höchste Klugheit . . .

Die Wildheit und Anarchie der Instinkte bei Sokrates ist ein décadence-Symptom.

Do not these quotations describe Rector Kleist as well? An eccentric, rather ridiculous little hunchback whose bearing, dress, etc. are excessive, whose instincts are in rebellion (for Nietzsche a sign of physical weakness), who detests himself and who possesses dialectical skill and *die höchste Klugheit?* As shown above, Kaiser himself linked Kleist with Socrates, obviously having in mind not Nietzsche's aphorism 340 but the Socrates Nietzsche more generally portrayed and despised as the embodiment of *ressentiment*. Kaiser views Kleist with more sympathy and understanding than Nietzsche does Socrates, but in most respects the two characters are as alike as two peas in a pod.

If we pause now to correlate the two plays discussed this far, their great similarity will readily be observed. Not only do they both embody the *Geist-Leben* motiv, and have corresponding sets of adversaries, but the ostensible platonic dichotomy is in both cases oriented along the lines of Nietzsche's polarity: healthy instinct versus dialectical rationality. This finding is significant for the entire period which these plays span (1903–1919), as many of the intervening plays likewise deal with the *Geist-Leben* motiv in the same Nietzschean sense and, in addition, are in some way directly indebted to Nietzsche himself. Thus, *Die jüdische Witwe* (1904), whose heroine knows no law but that of instinct and is a worthy offspring of Wedekind's Lulu and her kin, has as its motto the famous lines from *Also sprach Zarathustra*, "O meine Brüder, zerbrecht, zerbrecht mir die alten Tafeln!" In the play itself, the witty King Nebuchadnezzar ostensibly quotes his contemporary Zoroaster, but acutally parodies the style and tone of Nietzsche's popular work: "Siehe mit deiner Sternenseele den Mond an, wenn der blasse ins blaue Tuch der Nacht gezeichnet steht—also spricht Zarathustra" (I, 167). Judith's husband, Manasse, has much in common with Rector Kleist as he likewise embodies impotent intellectuality strongly desiring life, although Manasse is drawn more unsympathetically since he is not a victim but a perpetrator of bourgeois injustice. The antithesis is here further heightened by contrasting youth with old age.

Several years later Kaiser created a blood-brother to Manasse, although a bit more vindictive and neurotic, King Mark in *König Hahnrei* (1910); the young lovers, Tristan and Isolde, are the usual uneloquent and healthy representatives of virulent instinct.

Der Geist der Antike (1904) presents the customary dichotomy in terms of a professor of archeology who strives vainly to change his allegiance from scholarship to life. It is more than likely that Professor Nehrkorn was meant to be a humorous jibe at Nietzsche himself, as Nehrkorn, like Nietzsche, is a professor of classical antiquity who claims that prevailing views on antiquity need to be basically rectified in favor of a dionysiac interpretation. Nehrkorn says to his son, "Dein Vater schafft die Welt zum zweiten Mal" (V, 418), which Leo correctly interprets to mean, "Unsere Auffassung der Antike bedarf durchgreifender Korrektur?" (V, 418). Darkly, the professor exclaims, "Ich grub die Mumie der Welt aus" (V, 426). He is convinced that Leo has gained from the turbulent ocean the same insight into life that he has carried away from his studies in Greece:

> Leo, was sich dir im brausenden Orkan der Meere erschlossen hat—du wirst diesen Strom des heißen, jungen, ewig gegenwärtigen Lebens auch in Deinem Vaterhause nicht mehr entbehren. Ich trug ihn als beste Beute aus Hellas hier herein!— (V, 417)

Nehrkorn has other Nietzschean attitudes, disdaining the masses whom he terms "Schafsköpfe" dominated by illusions, "Blendwerk des Irrtums." He rejects scholarship and historical causality in the same manner that Nietzsche did in *Vom Nutzen und Nachteil der Historie für das Leben*. Nehrkorn says with regard to scholarship: "Leuchte der Wissenschaft—was ist denn das für ein Licht? Sternenlicht, wenn die Sonne erlosch—keine Hand wärmt sich daran. Nachtzeit! Nachtzeit!" (V, 426). He refuses to consider himself a part of the chain of events. Indignantly he snorts, "Ich schustre den Kalender nicht" (V, 425). And when Eck insists, "Wir alle hampeln an der eisernen Kette von gestern und heute," Nehrkorn retorts, "Als Hampelmann tun Sie das" (V, 425), meaning that only an unenlightened person could hold to such a naive view. His ideal is "das starke, mutige, fruchtbringende Leben" (V, 415). The title *Geist der Antike* is itself an ironic word-play on that theme, since the *Geist* in question is not *Geist* at all but dionysiac *Leben*.

Both *Leben* and *Geist* are mocked in the strongly anti-bourgeois comedy *Der Zentaur* (1906) in which the hero's pedantic devotion both to duty and to life is ridiculed as "übermenschlich": "Mir recken Sie sich hinten und vorne . . . übermenschlich! übermenschlich! Der Mythos wölkt sich um Sie, Zentaur! Zentaur!" (I, 294). *Die Versuchung* (1910) and *Von morgens bis mitternachts* (1912) are tragedies which deal with the quest for *Leben*. A clear victory is won by instinct over effete culture in the comedy, *Europa* (1914); the heroine—another Judith—prefers the masculine soldiers to the light-footed dancers.

Three dramas of the 1920's still utilize the *Leben-Geist* theme but the spirit of these plays is quite different from those of the earlier period. In *Kanzlist Krehler* (1921), the protagonist is another Kleist in conflict with a full-bosomed wife. However, the latter's bond with life is less instinct than a bourgeois desire for material possessions which has forced her husband to keep his nose to the grindstone—and miss out on life. In *Gats* (1924), the motif crops out at the end of the play; the secretary when faced with the choice between humanitarian birth control and having children, decides in favor of instinct and turns her idealistic lover—who has made her sterile—over to the police. *Lederköpfe* (1927) employs the conception of a treacherous soldier who deforms his head and covers it with a leather hood (made of animal skin!) as a brutal example of body without head, *Leben* without *Geist*.

It is no easy matter to describe in a few words Kaiser's gradual shift towards idealism. His popular expressionistic dramas of the second decade of the century furnish an accurate testimonial of his views concerning the destructive force of automation, capitalism and war on human personality, but in the main these dramas were sociological rather than philosophical, and their criticism was essentially a refinement of the social criticism found in his earlier plays. In the third decade, however, a new idealism became apparent (foreshadowed in *König Hahnrei*, 1910). Kaiser's protagonists now frequently rejected the ugly world of phenomena in favor of a mental world which conformed to their wishes. At times the flight was involuntary (*Zweimal Oliver*), at times belief proved stronger than the outwardly real world (*Oktobertag*).

This new idealism has frequently been associated with Kaiser's heightened interest in Plato, but such a view is only partly correct. Whereas Plato may have been an important factor in stimulating the new outlook, still Platonic idealism is essentially quite different from the subjectivism of Kaiser's characters. It would seem that Kaiser sought through Plato to overcome Nietzsche's nihilism without ever quite succeeding.

The essays written by Kaiser in the decade 1918–1929, although concerned primarily with the problem of his art, were filled with Nietzschean concepts.[27] To list a few such ideas: the world is chaotic and ruled by blind chance. Life is the sole meaning of existence. Man is the highest form of energy; he must assert himself against external forces and develop his potentialities to the full. "Der Mensch der Höchstleistung ist der Typ der Zeit, die morgen anfängt" (IV, 580). The goal of existence is "die Erneuerung des Menschen" (IV, 549).[28]

Since space is restricted and the material voluminous, our discussion will be confined to the key concept in Kaiser's new idealism: spiritualized love. Although such love was in itself obviously not Nietzschean, the attempt will be made to show that the world outlook on which it was posited was still largely derived from Nietzsche.

For Kaiser and his later protagonists, spiritualized love meant pure feeling not unlike the ideal of religious and yet erotic feeling to be found in the hymns of Novalis. This pure feeling, awakened by attraction to a member of the opposite sex, was esteemed both as immediate experience and as the feeling which the memory of the experience occasioned. Or, one might say that the feeling, although born of physical attraction, was thereafter able to survive on its own momentum—even, perhaps, into eternity.[29] Such pure feeling was the highest possession of man to be cherished and protected at all costs.

A good illustration of how spiritualized love combined the real and the ideal may be seen in the drama, *Die Flucht nach Venedig* (1922) wherein the physical desire of the heroine was spiritualized when she abandoned herself to it completely. Kaiser presented the thesis with his customary ironic distortion: George Sand was true to her lover for the first time when she betrayed him since, in sleeping with the Italian doctor, she had for the first time been true to Musset's ideal. This ideal—also Kaiser's—had been that love must entail complete self-abandonment; hitherto Sand had been accustomed to exploit her sexual experiences as a source of material for her novels. But now in the arms of another, she could preserve "die ewige Keuschheit des Empfindens" and later say to Musset, "Ich lebte für dich,

---

[27] Cf. particularly, "Dichtung und Energie" (1922), "Der Mensch im Tunnel" (1924), and "Die Sinnlichkeit des Gedankens" (1924).

[28] Cf. also Fix, pp. 33–40.

[29] At the close of *Bellerophon*, Apollo says, "Denn nur dies bedeutet die gewährte Erdenfrist: dir die Gefährtin zu erlesen für den einsamen Verein der Ewigkeit" (*Griechische Dramen*, Zurich, 1948), p. 376.

als ich diese Nacht erlebte" (II, 70). Not bourgeois conventions of loyalty, but intensity and purity of feeling were what mattered.

Virtually all of Kaiser's idealistic lovers derive their love from an initial physical attraction which is then sublimated into the realm of the spiritual—Juana, the wife of Claudius, Friedrich, the Countess Lavalette, Gilles, Vera, Elise, Adrienne, François, Agnete, Marie, Noelle, Rosamunde, among others. Even in *Oktobertag*, where the mind experiences its greatest victory and Catherine wills her dream into reality, there was an initial physical encounter that lit the flame of love. Sylvette in *Brand im Opernhaus* (1922) might seem to possess a truly spiritual love since it was awakened by the realization of the loftiness of her husband's feeling rather than by physical attraction. But a moment's reflection reveals that the husband's love, born of desire, was spiritualized passion and that Sylvette's love was a mirror of this passion. Awakened, she desired to be his wife in every sense of the word, and only when he refused to consider her as alive, did she commit suicide to preserve his dream. Her love is predicated on the fact of their marriage and physical bond.

The term spiritualized and not spiritual has been chosen to characterize Kaiser's new conception of love, since this feeling did not originate in a serene and inviolable realm of the absolute, and was not a pure love of God or virtue, but rather remained, as before, love between man and woman, born of the flesh, and only then rising into the world of spirit. The impetus for the new love still comes from the world of dionysiac reality and has its roots in *Leben*.

Because spiritualized love did not derive from an ideal world, but issued forth initially from the ugly reality of carnal desire, there existed an ever-present struggle between the ideal and the real, with the result that spiritual love is integrally related to and often characterized by suffering. No hard and fast line can be drawn as to the why and when of the suffering, but it is always correlated to the interplay of the two worlds. To speak with Schiller, the characters have little opportunity for *Anmut* and much for *Würde*. When they appear stonily serene like Rosamunde Floris and der Herr von ∴, they usually inflict suffering on others. For that matter, Rosamunde's serenity is indeed only a mask, as we shall see presently, and none of the other heroes possesses what might properly be termed serenity of spirit. In *Alain und Elise* (1938), Kaiser insisted that suffering was essential to the preservation of spiritualized love. Elise inflicted pain both on herself and her lover, Alain, having him unjustly incarcerated for life, to fan the precious flame of love. A love such as hers, she told Frocquenard, could thrive only in the deep shafts of suffering. In *Pygmalion* (1944), "göttlich Leiden" became the artist's "reichster Schatz" (VI, 597). We need not consider further the many protagonists who suffer in suppressing their own desire and sacrifice themselves at the altar of their love—they are almost legion—, and one notes again how closely Kaiser's new ideal is associated with the reality of dionysiac being.

When one considers the strong dionysiac undertones of Kaiser's idealism, coupled with the deeply pessimistic utterances of his most autobiographical protagonists, one wonders as to the strength of his idealistic convictions. Pygmalion was even more dejected than the dying Socrates as conceived by Kaiser, who at least had an ideal that might, perhaps, be realized. Pygmalion was forced to the grim conclusion that the ideal could never be brought to life. Napoleon in *Pferdewechsel* (1938) had little faith in his mission and only continued his tragic and lonely course in order not to betray the naive faith of a young widow. Kaiser, himself, at his trial for theft in 1921, stated that he had gone to such lengths to avoid the utter meanness of the world.[30] It would appear that Kaiser's idealism represented rather a flight from the engulfing reality of nihilism than a triumphant defeat of chaos, that Kaiser affirmed life less with the serene faith of Plato than in the tragic sense of Nietzsche's *amor fati*.

The insecurity implicit in Kaiser's idealism was also reflected in the radical manner in which the ideal was to be cherished and preserved. There is precious little of Platonic temperance in Kaiser's ethic; rather he employed with even greater extremism the Nietzschean master morality, the doctrine of "beyond good and evil," which he had utilized in his earlier plays. It will be remembered that Kleist and Socrates had limited their infractions of bourgeois morality to misleading dialectic and some outright lies while defending their cause. Judith had, to be sure, felt justified in murdering Manasse and Holofernes, but Kaiser presented her with a certain humorous irony which was missing in his later dramas. The later protagonists shy from no crimes when it is necessary to preserve their ideal.

Of the numerous examples at hand, one will suffice to illustrate the point. In *Rosamunde Floris* (1936), which Kaiser termed his "kühnste und vollkommenste Dichtung," the heroine is a girl with a voice that is "glokkenrein in der Seele" and resounds "aus Herzenstiefen." She has "die weißen Augen" found only in people "die nichts zu verbergen haben" (III, 379). Yet this pure girl commits every conceivable crime—slander, decep-

---

[30] *New York Times* (16 February 1921), p. 15.

tion, perjury, adultery, homicide, infanticide—in order to preserve her inner spark of love free from taint. Once she has achieved this end for all time, she confesses to a crime that she has *not* committed, so that may atone for the wrong she has done.

Rosamunde is no monster. She was fully aware of what is normally considered right and wrong and respected these values; she paid for her violation of traditional mores with her life. But she had seen through the veil of Maja and was aware of what was significant in life, the preservation of the ideal; she sacrificed everything to this end. The grotesque and ironic perspective of the drama is merely another manifestation of Kaiser's profound pessimism.

This ethical relativism can be all the more closely related with the immoralism of the superman, as Kaiser espoused the superman ideal itself ever since the end of World War I, identifying the superman with the tragic artist and so with himself.

At his trial Kaiser viewed himself as a superman, insisting that he was "the greatest living German poet" and "that his condemnation would mean a catastrophe for civilization." Kaiser contended that he was not "everybody," and consequently not "bound by ordinary laws."[31] If one is inclined to doubt the sincerity of these extreme utterances, one need only to recall the words of Athena in *Pygmalion*, assuring the artist that he is the misunderstood genius of mankind: "So seid Ihr Künstler Fremdlinge im Volk,/ Das lieber steinigt, als den Genius sieht" (VI, 522). Were it not for him, Athena told Pygmalion, Zeus would long since have destroyed mankind. It was the artist's lot to pursue a path of loneliness and suffering so that mankind might be redeemed—"in der Erlösertat für alle Menschen." The latter words might seem more suited to Christ than to Zarathustra, but it must be noted that Pygmalion, unlike Christ, had only contempt for the common herd of men.

Or one may refer to a typical artist like Abel Parr in *Vinzent verkauft ein Bild* (1937) who does not shy from fraud and deception, in the firm conviction that he belongs to the select few who stand above good and evil, and whose job it is "die Schöpfung zu vollenden. Denn das ist Kunst" (VI, 198).

The figure of Napoleon furnishes another clue to Kaiser's veneration of the superman. As Paulsen rightly says, the pacifist Kaiser's admiration for Napoleon even through the Hitler era is only comprehensible

---

[31] *New York Times* (16 February 1921), p. 15.

wenn man erkennt, daß Kaiser in Napoleon nicht in erster Linie den General und überhaupt nicht einen gewissenlosen Machtpolitiker sah, sondern das in der Geschichte einmal sichtbar gewordene schöpferische Prinzip, den Übermenschen aus Fleisch und Blut.[32]

As early as *Das Frauenopfer* (1915) and again in *Das Los des Ossian Balvesen* (1934), a noble Napoleon appears in the background. To be sure the comedy, *Napoleon in New Orleans* (1937–1938) condemns the *imperator* principle, but the earnest and autobiographical *Pferdewechsel* (1938) presents Napoleon in all his grandeur and dignity as a courageous martyr, a tragic hero, who has tread a hard and lonely path in a futile effort to demonstrate to herd-humanity what greatness really is. In this play Napoleon, the superman and Kaiser himself are closely linked. Paulsen's assumption seems well taken that the Napoleon plays of 1938 are related to the plans Kaiser made the following year for a Nietzsche play to be entitled *Ariadne*.[33]

As for the protagonists of the "idealistic" plays, it is not too much to claim that every one of them was, in his immoralism and dedication to an ideal, a superman seen through the distorting prism of Kaiser's irony. Even the early heroes of the pacifist dramas are supermen. The first of these, Eustache de Saint-Pierre, for example, is an unconventional hero who defies bourgeois notions of honor but is willing to lay down his life for his ideal.

Thus our final discussion has shown that Kaiser's ideal of spiritualized love rested on four Nietzschean concepts: 1) dionysiac reality 2) heroic suffering 3) ethical relativism 4) the superman ideal.

Let us recapitulate briefly before concluding. We have sought to show that during the period, 1903–1919, Kaiser's outlook lay rooted in the Nietzschean notion of dionysiac being, with many of the plays of the period dealing with the motiv, *Geist-Leben*, in the Nietzschean sense of healthy instinct versus dialectical rationality, and having other Nietzschean features as well. In the later period, Kaiser eulogized spiritualized love, but even this concept was predicated on the continued existence of the world of instinct.

---

[32] Paulsen, p. 107.

[33] A hint as to the possible content of *Ariadne* may be gained from Kaiser's contemporaneous play *Klawitter* (1938). In the latter play, Tibis cites Nietzsche and a short time after this, Hoff addresses his wife as Ariadne—a few moments before he learns that she has betrayed him. An unfaithful Ariadne in connection with the name of Nietzsche brings to mind Cosima Wagner. Hence it is likely that *Ariadne* was to deal with Nietzsche's relations to Cosima, perhaps during the "Triebchen" period, perhaps later when Nietzsche was on the verge of insanity and called her Ariadne.

Throughout the later period, Kaiser's idealism often seemed insecure, floating like a cockle-shell on an ocean of nihilism. After World War I Kaiser liked to conceive of himself as a tragic superman, waging single-handed the battle for humanity and practicing the master morality. All of his later protagonists are dedicated and ruthless supermen. It does not come as a surprise that Kaiser evinced strong interest in Nietzsche in the years 1938–1939.

Whether Kaiser is to be considered a Nietzschean is a matter of definition. Certainly Nietzsche in no way detracted from his originality. On the other hand, Nietzsche very definitely influenced his thinking, choice of motifs, characterization, and perhaps even the tone of his dramas and essays.[34]

Kaiser's relationship to Nietzsche is strikingly similar to that of other eminent German writers at the turn of the century who found themselves in a terrifying world deprived of absolute standards and ideals by means of which they might chart a meaningful course through life. Like Thomas Mann, Hermann Hesse, Franz Kafka and a host of others who felt themselves decadent artists unable to cope with brutal life—and were strengthened in their conviction by a familiarity with Nietzsche's doctrine—, Kaiser sought constantly within the framework of his artistic creation to come to terms with life—with his own life. The basic dichotomy, *Geist* versus *Leben*, which in essence concerned him from first to last, may freely be rendered as the idealist Georg Kaiser striving to cope with Nietzschean nihilism.

[34] For further discussion of Nietzschean influence on Kaiser, see Raymond English, "Ethics in the Works of Georg Kaiser: The Conflict between Individualism and Altruism" (Diss. University of North Carolina at Chapel Hill, expected completion date, fall 1975). The first half of the dissertation deals with Kaiser's individualistic ethic, including the extent to which it is derived from Nietzschean concepts such as vitality, the will to power, sublimation of Eros, the *Genie*, and the *Geniemoral*.

Nietzschean Influence in Musil's *Der Mann ohne Eigenschaften*

Any attempt to determine Nietzschean influence in *Der Mann ohne Eigenschaften*[1] should begin with a consideration of the central character, Ulrich, since the huge though fragmentary novel is ultimately concerned with his search for a purpose in life. The profound moral and eschatological implications of this quest may best be indicated by giving a brief synopsis of the story.

Prior to the time of the narrative, Ulrich had given up a promising career as an officer when he came to identify military life with romantic idealism. Subsequently, he had given up an equally promising career as a mathematician when he decided that science and technology were destroying "Seele" and dehumanizing western culture. However, despite this rejection of reason and order, his trained intellect remained suspicious of tempting ventures into the irrational, with the result that he became an uncertain, passive and cynical observer. This is the Ulrich the reader first encounters. Ulrich's indecision and confusion ultimately lead him to set aside one year in which to determine whether life can be meaningful. In the course of this experiment, which is the actual concern of the novel, he investigates several widely divergent, utopian possibilities.

---

[1] Robert Musil, *Gesammelte Werke*, I (Hamburg, 1952), 1672 ff. This edition of the novel contains the fragment published earlier by Musil as well as a number of hitherto unpublished fragments. Henceforth, in this study, page references to the novel will be given in parentheses, usually in the text of the paper, without further bibliographical data. For the sake of simplicity we have assigned volume numbers to the other volumes in the *Gesammelte Werke* based on the order of their publication: II = *Tagebücher, Aphorismen, Essays und Reden;* III = *Prosa, Dramen und späte Briefe*. References to these volumes will include the volume number. For additional information concerning the unpublished manuscripts, we have relied on *Robert Musil: Eine Einführung in das Werk* by Ernst Kaiser and Eithne Wilkins (Stuttgart, 1962), henceforth referred to as *KW*. Occasional references to *KW* does not mean that we are in full agreement with all of its conclusions. We do not comment on the other critical Musil literature (Allesch, Bachmann, Boehlich, Braun, Grenzmann, Pike, Rasch, Sokel, Zak, etc.) as it has limited itself either to a laconic affirmation of Nietzschean influence or to a brief reference to Clarisse as a superficial Nietzschean.

The first of these utopias is correlated with an attitude of dionysiac abandon. Although important to Achilles and Anders, as the hero was variously called in early versions of the novel, the dionysiac solution to life's problems appeals to Ulrich only on rare occasions and he usually considers it a dangerous seduction leading to insanity.

He gives more serious consideration to the second possibility, termed the "Utopie des Essayismus," which is a rational attempt based on Nietzschean relativism to straddle and bracket ever more closely the unattainable truth. However, when no positive results seem forthcoming, Ulrich turns again to irrationalism and, together with his twin sister Agathe, seeks to attain a mystical serenity in the "Utopie des andern Lebens," based on an attempt to blend platonic and erotic love. During the course of his involvement with this obviously antisocial utopia, treated in the novel in a section entitled "Die Verbrecher" and rooted in Nietzschean immoralism, Ulrich becomes disillusioned with subjective ethics and terms them a passing fad. According to later fragments, the paradisiacal existence *à deux* turns out unsatisfactorily, and a third utopia, termed the "induktive Gesinnung," is envisioned which once again is socially directed and takes into account the daily problems of existence and the need for getting along with one's fellow men. Nevertheless, even in this final utopia, certain basic Nietzschean elements are in evidence, such as the dual morality which distinguishes between the masses and the inspired few.

Whereas none of these utopias directly reflect Nietzsche's *Weltanschauung*, all are presented in a Nietzschean framework. This study will concern itself with an examination of the Nietzschean elements in Musil's novel.

To begin with Ulrich then, he has been endowed with many traits of the Nietzschean superman. In his youth he strove to be "so etwas wie ein Fürst oder Herr des Geistes" (156), and kept his body as strong and supple as a panther's (47). The thirty–two–year old Ulrich presented in the novel has retained most of these features, mitigated only by a strong dash of nihilistic irony:

> Mit der seelischen Beweglichkeit . . . verbindet sich bei ihm noch eine gewisse *Angriffslust*. Er ist ein männlicher Kopf. Er ist *nicht empfindsam für andere Menschen* und hat sich selten in sie hineinversetzt, außer um sie für seine Zwecke kennen zu lernen. *Er achtet Rechte nicht, wenn er nicht den achtet, der sie besitzt*, und das geschieht selten. Denn es hat sich mit der Zeit eine gewisse *Bereitschaft zur Verneinung* in ihm entwickelt, eine biegsame Dialektik des Gefühls, die ihn leicht dazu verleitet, *in etwas, das gut geheißen*

wird, einen Schaden zu entdecken, dagegen *etwas Verbotenes zu verteidigen* und Pflichten mit dem Unwillen abzulehnen, der aus dem *Willen zur Schaffung eigener Pflichten* hervorgeht. Trotz dieses Willens überläßt er aber seine moralische Führung mit gewissen Ausnahmen, die er sich gestattet, einfach jenem ritterlichen Anstand, der in der bürgerlichen Gesellschaft so ziemlich alle Männer leitet, solange sie in geordneten Verhältnissen leben und führt auf diese Weise *mit dem Hochmut, der Rücksichtslosigkeit und Nachlässigkeit eines Menschen, der zu seiner Tat berufen ist,* das Leben eines anderen Menschen, der von seinen Neigungen und Fähigkeiten einen mehr oder weniger gewöhnlichen und sozialen Gebrauch macht. (155 [my italics])

From this passage it is evident that Ulrich possesses the Nietzschean characteristics of masculinity and aggressiveness, disdain for pity, egotistical self-esteem, respect only for equals and not for traditions; that he is endowed with a nihilistic propensity, a distrust of the good and an attraction to the forbidden, a dislike for social duties and a will to create his own duties; that he is imbued with arrogance, ruthlessness, indifference, and a strong sense of mission. Ulrich's two prototypes in early versions of the novel mentioned above, Achilles and Anders, consider themselves to be a kind of "little Napoleon," who under other circumstances might have become a Mongolian general (*KW*, 137). Despite their cynicism, however, all three protagonists are filled with an intense desire to improve mankind. Thus, one early fragment significantly bore the title, *Der Erlöser,* and while still a young man Ulrich had viewed the world as a great laboratory, "wo die besten Arten, Mensch zu sein, durchgeprobt und neue entdeckt werden müßten" (156). It will be shown presently that a new morality becomes Ulrich's main concern.

As the title of the novel suggests, Ulrich is a complete relativist who distrusts all such concepts as *Geist, Seele* and *Leben,* analyzing them endlessly without ever reaching satisfactory conclusions. What he says in the abstract of *Geist* holds for his own intellectual outlook: "Er hält kein Ding für fest, kein Ich, keine Ordnung; weil unsre Kenntnisse sich mit jedem Tag ändern können, glaubt er an keine Bindung, und alles besitzt den Wert, den es hat, nur bis zum nächsten Akt der Schöpfung, wie ein Gesicht, zu dem man spricht, während es sich mit den Worten verändert" (158). He even considers the possibility that the dissolution of the ego may be imminent (144).

Such relativism is closely related to nihilism, and so it is not surprising to find that Ulrich holds the world to be devoid of goal or meaning. In his reflections concerning the world as a great laboratory, he had continued:

"Daß das Gesamtlaboratorium etwas planlos arbeitete, und daß die Leiter und die Theoretiker des Ganzen fehlten, gehörte auf ein anderes Blatt" (156). Ulrich is of the opinion that mankind is in a transitional state that may endure till the last days of our planet. To comfort his friend Walter, he expresses the conviction that mankind is rapidly approaching a utopia, but admits to himself that "dieser Jugendtraum längst hohl geworden war, den er Walter vorhielt" (222). Walter senses Ulrich's true attitude. "Und wir sollen auf jeden Sinn des Lebens verzichten?" he asks. Ulrich can only counter with the equivocating query, "wozu er eigentlich einen Sinn brauche?" (222).

After his pessimistic meditations on *Geist*, Ulrich had asked himself why he had not become a pilgrim, commenting, "Wer das Leben nicht bejahen will, sollte wenigstens das Nein des Heiligen sagen" (157).

Ulrich's nihilism encompasses an awareness of Nietzsche's concept of the eternal recurrence. At the death of his father, which occurs significantly between two utopian adventures, Ulrich is plunged into a darkly pessimistic mood. Looking at his dead father's face, he senses the possibility that everything is only an eternal repetition and circular movement of the mind: "Vielleicht war alles darin, die Rasse, die Gebundenheit, das Nichtpersönliche, der Strom des Erbgangs, in dem man nur eine Kräuselung ist, die Einschränkung, Entmutigung, das ewige Wiederholen und im Kreis Gehen des Geistes, das er im tiefsten Lebenswillen haßte!" (708).[2]

When Ulrich is toying with the notion of suicide, he detects in the recurrence of a *Lieblingsbild*—experienced in the same dreamlike state in which Nietzsche had his vision of the eternal recurrence—"eine seltsame Übereinstimmung und ein sonderbares Zusammentreffen" (678), and then sees himself as a series of puppets with broken springs (679). Kaiser and Wilkins relate this vision to young Musil's comment written after the failure of his first novel: "Gewisse Erinnerungen treten plötzlich in das Gedächtnis und man ahnt einen eisernen Zusammenhang" (*KW*, 192). In a fragment entitled "Atemzüge eines Sommertages," Ulrich holds to the idea of the eternal recurrence in association with other Nietzschean viewpoints:

---

[2] *KW* comments as follows on this passage: "Und wenn *plus ça change, plus c'est la même chose* wirklich alles ist, was sein kann, und der letzte geistige Gewinn aus all den Jahren, in welchen 'Der Mann ohne Eigenschaften' entstand, nur eine 'Welt ohne feste Form' ist, eingeschlossen in den Reifen der ewigen Wiederkehr in jenen [sic] wiederkehrenden Alptraum, den Nietzsche, der bewunderte Lehrmeister des Logikers Anders, träumte, warum sollte dann Ulrich widerstehen?" (p. 203). In a fragment dated by Frisé around 1934, Ulrich terms Nietzsche "sein eigener Lehrer" (1379).

"Dem appetitartigen Teil der Gefühle verdankt die Welt alle Werke und alle Schönheit, allen Fortschritt aber auch alle Unruhe, und zuletzt all ihren *sinnlosen Kreislauf*" (1174 [my italics]).

The tragic realization of life's futility imbues Ulrich and his predecessors with a deep sense of isolation. Monsieur le vivisecteur,[3] the first prototype, feels that he is frozen deep under polar ice (*KW*, 49), a close parallel to Nietzsche's icy high noon of revelation or the icy wastes referred to in his poem "Vereinsamt."[4] Ulrich is more communicative than the others, but he is still a lone wolf, unmarried and unemployed, who contemplates life with passive irony.

Paradoxically enough, but like his forerunners and like Nietzsche, Ulrich remains deeply concerned with the need for a complete revaluation of moral values.[5] He rejects conventional morality as "die Altersform eines Kräftesystems" (258) and feels the necessity, "eine Moral, die seit zweitausend Jahren immer nur im kleinen dem wechselnden Geschmack angepaßt worden ist, in den Grundlagen zu verändern" (259). His radical proposal entails the elimination of moral codes entirely, as he is of the opinion that codification leads to rigidity and loss of moral essence (258, 779). In an established society, virtues soon become as unbearable as vices (258). Ulrich cannot help but feel that there is nothing more useless than a person good on principle alone (764, 780). Anders had expressed the same idea more vigorously, insisting that "Fortschritt kommt nur durch das Böse."[6] In the aforementioned fragment, Ulrich observes that human action is largely determined by instincts which are ambivalent in their relation to good and evil (1175), and in a related fragment discusses masculine, anti-Christian egotism as the source of all moral values:

[3] Nietzsche referred in *Genealogie der Moral* to "Vivisektoren des Geistes" (*Werke in 4 Bänden*, ed. Karl Schlechta [Munich, 1954 ff.], II, 842).

[4] Hermann Hesse referred to this poem in his novel *Steppenwolf* (1927) to illustrate the isolation of the genius.

[5] Nietzsche used the concept of nihilism variously, at times to mean a completely negative position that viewed the world as devoid of meaning, more frequently to refer to a complete dissolution and relativizing of values which served him as a starting point for establishing a new set of values. Both Musil and Nietzsche vacillated between these two attitudes.

[6] *KW*, 137. Concerning Ander's philosophy, *KW* adds in parentheses, "von der es in Notizen heißt, daß sie auf Nietzsche beruht." Commenting on the unpublished *Erlöser* manuscript, *KW* states, "Sein [Ulrich's] Vorläufer Anders versuchte seine Vorliebe für Moosbrugger philosophisch auf Gedanken Nietzsches, des 'bewunderten Lehrmeisters,' zu begründen" (p. 169).

. . . wer sich nicht selbst liebe, könne nicht gut sein, eine Botschaft, die ziemlich das Gegenteil vom Christentum ist! Denn nicht, wer gegen andre gut ist, gilt als gut; sondern wer gut an sich selbst ist, ist es notwendig gegen andre. Das ist also eine schöpferische Art Selbstliebe ohne Schwäche und Unmännlichkeit, eine kriegerische Übereinstimmung von Glück und Tugend, eine Tugend in stolzem Sinn. (1192)

Just as Zarathustra detests the notion of the smugly virtuous "letzte Mensch" who steers a careful middle course to avoid exertion, Ulrich disdains the modern tendency to regard strong feeling as psychopathic (259). He dreads to think what it would mean for "das gesunde Leben" were morality to consist of an anxious "mittleren Zustand zwischen zwei Übertreibungen . . . wenn sein [des Lebens] Ideal wirklich nichts anders als die Leugnung der Übertreibung seiner Ideale wäre" (259).

True morality must take into account the flux of reality, the "Beweglichkeit der Tatsachen" (259). It has to recognize that reason cannot probe the depths of "das wahre Leben." According to Ulrich, morality lies not in conduct according to rules but in carrying out one's acts "mit ganzer Seele." Any act is morally valid if committed "aus dem ganzen Wesen heraus." Morality is "ein ganz Begreifen" that transcended intellect and feeling (262).

These views held by Ulrich at the beginning of the experimental year are still quite strong in him months later during the first period of his life with Agathe, when he sums up his views in the following manner:

Ich glaube, daß alle Vorschriften unserer Moral Zugeständnisse an eine Gesellschaft von Wilden sind. Ich glaube, daß keine richtig sind. . . . Ich glaube, man kann mir tausendmal aus den geltenden Gründen beweisen, etwas sei gut oder schön, es wird mir gleichgültig bleiben, und ich werde mich einzig und allein nach dem Zeichen richten, ob mich seine Nähe steigen oder sinken macht. Ob ich davon zum Leben geweckt werde oder nicht. (786–87)

Although he then hesitates for a moment, admitting that he is unable to prove anything and that such an ambiguous position could lead to dangerous confusion, he goes on to say: "Ich glaube aber vor allem nicht an die Bindung von Bös durch Gut, die unser Kulturgemisch darstellt: das ist mir widerwärtig! Ich glaube also und glaube nicht!" (787)

To emphasize the invalidity of conventional mores, Ulrich frequently discusses murder, which in bourgeois eyes is conceived as the extreme crime. For him the fifth commandment does not represent "eine Wahrheit" and is not to be taken as an inviolable law (261). Not only are there valid exceptions to this law but in less clearly defined cases the reactions of the average newspaper reader are often in part sympathetic, vacillating between "Abscheu und Verlockung" (261). The act itself is not what matters, since a murder may be either a crime or a heroic deed (257). The decisive factor is whether one acted from inner necessity or not, since a truly moral person could never let himself be guided by an external law: "Er könnte glücklich sein, weil er nicht tötet, oder glücklich sein, weil er tötet, aber er könnte niemals der gleichgültige Eintreiber einer an ihn gestellten Forderung sein" (262; cf. 749).

Imbued with this attitude, Ulrich is able to contemplate murdering his arch-opponent, the pseudo-idealist Arnheim. Later, with Agathe, Ulrich adopts a somewhat more conservative attitude, but when she asks what he might do after committing murder, he is at first tempted to answer in good Nietzschean fashion: "Ich könnte ja vielleicht dadurch befähigt werden, ein Gedicht zu schreiben, das Tausenden das innere Leben gibt, oder auch eine große Erfindung zu machen" (751). When speaking of egotism, Ulrich had commented, "Ein guter Mann kann auch töten" (1196).

The morality of murder is embodied most clearly in the case of the sex-murderer Moosbrugger, which constitutes an earlier and more significant motif than the much discussed Collateral Campaign; the latter was, by the author's own admission, only a development of the Moosbrugger motif permitting the introduction of additional characters (KW, 141).[7]

When the strong, benign-looking carpenter Moosbrugger committed murder, he acted in harmony with his innermost need. An abnormal upbringing had made him extremely shy in the presence of women and this shyness later developed into an insane fear, inducing him to react in a frenzied and sadistic manner when approached by a prostitute. He came to believe that he was being persecuted by female spirits and ultimately sought refuge in insanity. The law court, with its psychiatric staff, sentences Moos-

---

[7] The Collateral Campaign has as its function to organize a celebration, to be held in 1918, of the seventieth anniversary of Franz Josef's accession to the throne. The purpose was to outdo the Prussians who were preparing to commemorate the thirtieth anniversary of William II in the same year. The long and futile search by the organizers of the Collateral Campaign for something worthy of celebrating is correlated with Ulrich's search for a meaning in life.

brugger to death for slaying a prostitute, but Ulrich is convinced that "immoralists" such as Luther and Meister Eckhart would have judged the case in a more profound manner and set the carpenter free (124–25).

Moosbrugger has both a passive and an active function in the novel. He not only serves to point up criticism of existing society and mores, but on the symbolical plane he also offers a solution to man's dilemma. Indeed, grotesque as it may seem, he represents the first irrational utopia Ulrich considers, a release from the stultifying bonds of reason and moral responsibility into frenzied dionysiac abandon, so well described by Nietzsche in *Die Geburt der Tragödie*. Clarisse and, to a lesser extent, Ulrich and Bonadea, see in Moosbrugger an answer to the problem of decadent civilization.[8]

Clarisse links Moosbrugger with the ecstatic mood of dionysiac music which Musil, like Nietzsche, distrusted for its enervating effect on the will to live.[9] Clarisse, it will be remembered, is a vigorous young pianist who thrills unduly to rapturous music and whose greatest wish is to continue to play endlessly (149). When Ulrich gives her a set of Nietzsche's works, she becomes a confirmed if superficial Nietzschean, advocating will and genius (50, 623). Now, more than ever, she exults in frenzied dreams of perfection, so that her husband fears for her sanity and hates Ulrich for encouraging her to yield to this heady seduction (69).

It is only when Clarisse becomes convinced that Moosbrugger is musical that she becomes intensely interested in him and seeks his release (310, 445, 727). She now endeavors to enlist Ulrich's support in freeing the murderer, commenting, "du würdest verwandelt werden" (223). In addition, she writes a letter to Count Leinsdorf suggesting that the Collateral Action be celebrated as a Nietzsche year and closes her letter with an appeal that something be done for Moosbrugger (233; cf. 303, 361, 453).

The point is obvious. Freeing the insane murderer is for her equivalent to freeing the dionysiac forces within herself. Like Ulrich, a nihilist who does not balk at murder,[10] Clarisse sees in such self-abandonment an escape

---

[8] Musil does not refer in the published version to Moosbrugger's code of action as a utopia, presumably because he had by this time come to reject such a radical cure for the world's ills. It will be seen, however, that even Ulrich regards Moosbrugger at times as a utopian possibility.

[9] Musil wrote in 1902, after attending a concert by Paderewski: "Wenn man Jemanden hätte, der einem fort und fort solcherweise die Seele umspinnen würde oder selbst so wäre. —Ich empfand, daß ich mich ganz vom Leben abwenden und ganz diesem zuwenden würde,—weil das *Leben* nicht im Stande ist, mir etwas Gleichwertiges zu bieten" (*KW*, 70–71).

[10] Clarisse says to Ulrich, ". . . ist das Leben, das wir führen, nicht furchtbar traurig?

from the emptiness of modern civilized life and a revitalizing force for an enervated culture.

To stress this point, the author lets Clarisse experience a strange daydream while playing the piano with Walter in their usual violent style. Depressed by thoughts of her past life, she abandons herself to the music and imagines that Moosbrugger's prison opens up before her like a refuge. She enters, filled with trepidation but encouraging herself—as she had done on an earlier occasion—with the thought, "Man muß bis zum Ende Musik machen!" Whereupon the cell becomes suffused with her being (Ich) which is likened to a delicious sense of intoxication: ". . . ein so mildes Gefühl wie eine Wundersalbe, aber als sie es für immer festhalten wollte, fing es an, sich zu öffnen und auseinanderzuschieben wie ein Märchen oder ein Traum." She now sees Moosbrugger sitting before her and sets about removing his fetters. "Während sich ihre Finger bewegten, kam Kraft, Mut, Güte, Schönheit, Reichtum in die Zelle . . ." The murderer is magically transformed into "ein schöner Jüngling" and she into "eine wunderbar schöne Frau" (150).

Freeing Moosbrugger symbolizes the release of the demonic and irrational forces in man, both as a protest against insipid bourgeois culture and as a revitalizing process. Musil's doubts as to the feasibility of such an irrational code of action are, of course, evident at many points in the novel and particularly in the fact that his savior is a wildly insane murderer and the savior's prophet a frenetic young woman (whom the author at times caricatures in brutal fashion). On the other hand, it cannot be overlooked that even in the published fragment Ulrich was on occasion sorely tempted by Moosbrugger's drastic solution. To cite the most telling example, one evening, despondent over the problems besetting him, Ulrich feels a sudden urge to leave his brightly illuminated house (i.e., the security of his rational self) to take a walk in the garden. Outside, the darkness ominously suggests to him the gigantic shape of Moosbrugger and the trees seem imbued with a strange plasticity. Although they appear wet and ugly as worms—an obvious symbolism for the underlying instincts—he can scarcely resist the desire to kneel down and embrace them, tears streaming over his face (264).

In the present context Ulrich's behavior implies more than nihilistic surrender. It will be remembered that his predecessors saw in Moosbrugger a symbol of positive action. Anders considered Moosbrugger to be the

Es kommt weder Gott noch Teufel. So gehe ich schon jahrelang herum" (674). She had calmly suggested to Walter that he murder Ulrich (364, 455; cf. also 627–28).

mirror of certain traits within himself while Achilles felt that the murderer was *his complete mirror image* (*KW*, 139). Ulrich cannot be completely detached from these earlier protagonists, since even he senses a close bond with Moosbrugger. When the carpenter is sentenced, Ulrich has the feeling that the murderer's fate means more to him than his own life (124). Earlier the idea occurred to Ulrich that if mankind as a whole could synthesize its dreams it would produce Moosbrugger, which is just another way of saying that Ulrich also views the condemned man as a savior (78). Nor should it be forgotten that Ulrich shares the insane carpenter's aversion to sexual relations and can readily understand that a man might seek to stifle a woman's shrieks by stuffing clods of dirt in her mouth (72).[11]

Another important character related to Moosbrugger is the nymphomaniac Bonadea, who personifies the sexual element in the dionysiac mood. She wants Ulrich to help free Moosbrugger, i.e., to identify himself with the latter, as she would like Ulrich to assume the murderer's innocence and sense of irresponsibility (590). Like Moosbrugger, Bonadea violates conventional morality without remorse and from a consuming desire. She seeks to convert Ulrich to her own sensuality and wants him to follow his instincts (594). Ulrich is enticed by the possibility she offers and "fühlte große Sehnsucht nach diesem Schlüpfrig-Schleirigen, nach Nachgeben und Vergessen" (595), but manages to resist. The orgiastic element is linked to Moosbrugger in an earlier fragment by having Clarisse incite Anders through her demoniacal piano-playing to seduce her, after which he feels committed to help free the murderer.[12]

The Moosbrugger motif, perhaps all-important in the earliest versions of the novel, recedes into the background of the later versions when confronted with the more serene utopia embodied in Ulrich's sister, Agathe, whose garden is light and friendly, and whose escape into a mystical "anderen Zustand" offers bliss comparable to platonic love (923). This rather erotic spiritual union bears a striking resemblance to the ideal of love

[11] Musil vacillates in a confusing manner, generally regarding Moosbrugger's solution as that of an insane mind, but then again identifying the murderer to a degree with Ulrich himself. Without a knowledge of the earlier versions, one would be inclined to conclude that Moosbrugger represents a dangerous nihilistic seduction rather than a utopian possibility.

[12] (*KW*, 171–72). Unpublished manuscript of 1905. In an even earlier fragment, music, eroticism, and dionysiac ecstasy were linked by having an errant wife dressed in a negligé receive the hero in a room containing a huge grand piano and a dionysiac mask (*KW*, 56).

found in some of Georg Kaiser's later plays.[13] However, our attention will here be directed to Agathe's Nietzschean characteristics.

Ulrich's charming sister also possesses the "eine Tugend" praised by Zarathustra, that complete harmony between act and intent which Musil termed "ein ganz Begreifen." Like Moosbrugger, she embodies an ideal of the irrational and the instinctive, and has a fair share of Bonadea's earthy sensuality, being only more passive and serene. She has had an unhappy second marriage and shares Ulrich's nihilistic views and his desire to escape the misery of daily existence (747). The two spend countless hours discussing questions of morality, during which time Agathe comes to accept Ulrich's relativistic *Lebensmoral*, largely because it articulates what she already believes.[14]

Without a twinge of conscience, Agathe commits what normally would be considered a serious crime; she forges her father's last will and testament. She does so to prevent her husband from sharing in her inheritance and possibly interfering with her present way of life. From her point of view her act is entirely justified, but the theorist Ulrich is horrified, chiding her that even Nietzsche had adjured his "freie Geister" to adhere to certain outer laws so that they might maintain their inner freedom (812). But when Agathe remains unmoved Ulrich decides to let destiny take its course, in the hope that the morality "des Steigens und Sinkens" would prove as applicable as "die einfache der Ehrlichkeit" (845). He was, as usual, torn between the compulsions of the law-making intellect and the law-breaking soul. On the one hand, he reasons that he is only a theoretical defender of evil who in practice leads a law-abiding existence and who has, so to speak, merely protected the idea of evil from the actual evildoers (843). At the moment he feels strongly drawn to the course of good (842). On the other hand, he has to admit to himself that he is better disposed after committing a conventionally wrong act, and that evil leads to a fuller development of one's faculties than does routine observance of good (839). In a decadent civilization such as he feels presently to exist (843), evil acts could on occasion not only be "ursprünglicher und kraftvoller . . . sondern geradezu moralischer" (841). In fact, in such a civilization good and bad become almost meaningless concepts when applied to an act committed "aus einer reinen, tiefen und ursprünglichen Handlungsweise" (841). Although Agathe's act violates moral law, it presents ˙eine betörende

---

[13] Cf. my essay, "Nietzsche and Georg Kaiser" in this volume, pp. 51–72.

[14] (764–88); cf. also 758, 762. Agathe says, "Ich möchte Hagauer umbringen."

Verlockung . . . , sobald man es mitträumte, denn dann entschwand alles Strittige und Geteilte, und es bildete sich der Eindruck einer leidenschaftlichen, bejahenden, zum Handeln drängenden Güte. . . ." (842). He cannot bring himself to condemn Agathe since her act represents a sincere and wholehearted attempt to achieve a "Zustand . . . , worin es eine Moral ohne Unterbrechung gibt" (845).

In an earlier version, the forgery had been only the first of a series of crimes perpetrated by Agathe and Anders as a kind of Nietzschean experiment in immoralism which ended in a short-lived incestuous paradise on a Mediterranean island (1443–67). In the published version of 1932, the episode is virtually terminated when Agathe's husband, Hagauer, in his letter accuses his wife of being "das strikteste Gegenteil einer ins Leben gerichteten und seiner kundigen Menschenart" (972). The latter, who had committed her misdeed in "einem einbildungsreichen Rauschzustand," now experiences "eine unbeschreibliche Nüchternheit" (974), and soon thereafter attempts suicide. Ulrich also has a change of heart and is now definitely convinced that she has been in the wrong. Even though morality in the present-day world is either in dissolution or in "Krämpfen," he insists that one should keep pure for the sake of a world yet to come (978). He abhors evil, he discovers, and views his earlier enthusiams for nihilism and immoralism as part of a passing fad:

> Ich selbst habe auch ursprünglich gedacht, daß man zu allem Nein sagen müsse; alle haben so gedacht, die heute zwischen fünfundzwanzig und fünfundvierzig sind; aber das war natürlich nur eine Art Mode: ich könnte mir vorstellen, daß jetzt bald der Umschwung und mit ihm eine Jugend kommt, die sich statt der Unmoral wieder die Moral ins Knopfloch stecken wird. (979)

Nietzsche's ideas are apparently rejected in both versions of the attempted flight into the mystical *tausendjährige Reich*, but even here Nietzschean nihilism and immoralism remain the central theme. Agathe embodies these concepts just as all the other characters mentioned, excluding at times the vacillating Ulrich.

Concerning Musil's rejection of certain aspects of Nietzsche and Nietzscheanism, it would appear that the mystical Austrian wanted to dissociate his interest in Nietzsche completely from the customary will to power interpretation of the latter. To this end he introduced into the story the Nietzschean writer Meingast, presumably a caricature of Ludwig Klages, who comes down from "Zarathustras Bergen" to spend several weeks with

Walter and Clarisse. In his advocacy of an irrational hierarchy based solely on power, Meingast is presented as a pompous, superficial and lascivious person whom Ulrich disdains as a "Schwätzer" (857).

An even more comprehensive rejection of Nietzsche seems implicit in the disillusionment experienced by Ulrich and Clarisse in the insane asylum, where the orgiastic exhibitionism of the insane brutally ridicules the romantic idea of dionysiac ecstasy. One inmate is actually an ironic portrayal of the insane Nietzsche. He is described as a man in his late fifties, obviously from the upper class, with bushy hair and a spiritualized face. His sickness is depressive *dementia paralytica*; the psychiatrist Siegmund whispers to Clarisse, "Ein alter Syphilitiker. Versündigungs- und nihilistische Wahnideen" (1004). The ironically drawn representative of Austrian militarism, General Stumm von Bordwehr, is deeply impressed by the serenity of the old man's face and feels compelled to remark, "die leibhaftige Geistesschönheit," but the accompanying physician throws cold water on this notion, explaining that the spiritualized expression resulted from a pathological relaxing of the facial muscles (1004).

To judge from the novel as published by the author, it would appear that Musil had gone the way of many other writers of his generation, such as Thomas Mann, Hermann Hesse, Stefan George and Georg Kaiser, who were at first captivated by the possibilities inherent in the new immoralism but who gradually became suspicious of an anarchistic morality. If one also takes the early fragments into consideration, the hero may be seen to have evolved from a Cesare Borgia type of ruthless superman to a mystical immoralist who ultimately rejects Nietzscheanism as a passing fad.

The published portion and early fragments comprise, however, only a part of Musil's work on the novel; there are also the later fragments on which he continued to work until his death in 1942. One cannot disregard these fragments on the ground that they were not final copy or that they were not published by the author himself, since Musil had wanted to publish more of the novel and was thwarted by lack of funds, the Nazi ban on his writings, and the difficulties of emigré existence.

In these later fragments there are indications that Musil contemplated having his hero explore the possibilities of a third utopia. We cannot attempt here to deal with the difficult and much disputed problem of whether the third utopia of the inductive attitude (*induktive Gesinnung*) was a continuation of the first or second utopia, or indeed of both. The scholars who have studied the manuscripts most intently, Frisé, Bausinger and the Kaiser-Wilkins team, at least agree that the fragments dealing with the third utopia are late fragments and that this utopia was to be the final utopian possibility to be considered. Now, whatever these fragmentary outlines and preliminary studies may fail to show, they do reveal a continued or renewed preoccupation with Nietzschean concepts; if these fragments are to be taken at all seriously, they indicate that Ulrich's rejection of Nietzsche either had little duration or reflected in essence a transition to a more mature approach to Nietzsche.

According to one late fragment, the utopia of the inductive attitude was to make a clear distinction between the morality for the many and the morality for the few (1621). The distinctly Nietzschean flavor of such a dual morality is further enhanced by the fact that the elite few were to utilize Ulrich's *Geniemoral* (1621). Even the morality for the many has Nietzschean overtones, as the following precepts demonstrate:

Zusatz 3: Zur Moral für die vielen gehört auch: das Mehrseinmüssen, als man ist.
Zusatz 4: Die wirkliche Welt braucht am meisten die Erfindung und Darlegung des "guten Bösen." (1623)

It may be noted in passing, that a fragment of 1932 dealing with the structure of the second book expands the second of these precepts to form the main motif of the novel: "*Im Ganzen* muß der Roman wohl *das 'gute Böse' erfinden und darlegen*, da es die Welt mehr braucht, als die utopische 'gute Güte'" (1633 [author's italics]).

The morality for the many is discussed in such Nietzschean terms as *Dekadenz, Ressentiment, Macht*, and *das Böse* (1622–26). Nietzsche is himself frequently referred to, in one instance three times on one page (1625). In commenting on the positive attributes of a use of force, Musil had Nietzsche very much in mind:

Die Produktion von Machtmenschen, die alles ihren Zwecken beugen, ist der Trick der Menschheit, ihre Zwecke zu erfüllen. So Nietzsche. . . . Positiv wirken die hauptsächlich von Nietzsche beschriebenen Tugenden der Macht: Stolz, Härte, Ausdauer, Mut, Geltenlassen, Neidfreiheit, Großzügigkeit, Gelassenheit, und so weiter. [Note the striking parallel to the earlier description of Ulrich!] Meist sind das auch Tugenden des Geistes. Siehe die Entwicklung des europäischen Geistes aus dem Kriegergeist. . . . Diesem wurde (nach Nietzsche) das fremde, vergiftende Element des Christentums zugesetzt. (1625)

To be sure, Nietzsche is considered only as one alternative and Musil then raises the question whether evil is unavoidable and to be esteemed (1625–

26). Significantly, however, he leaves the question open.

Late references in Musil's diary also indicate a continued interest in Nietzsche. Presumably in 1937, Musil asked himself the question, "Habe ich in meiner Jugend auch nur ein Drittel von ihm aufgenommen?" and answered amazed, "Und doch entscheidenden Einfluß" (II, 401). In the margin adjoining an early comment reading, "Nietzsche an sich hat keinen großen Wert," he later jotted, "jugendliche Anmaßung" (II, 43).

Until the many questions concerning Musil's *Nachlaß* are clearly resolved one cannot, of course, make definitive statements about his later attitude. But it seems reasonably certain that Nietzschean ideas would have formed a cornerstone of the entire work, had the novel been completed.

In conclusion two ancillary points may briefly be touched upon. There is little doubt that the novel expresses Musil's own basic viewpoints. This is apparent both in the autobiographical nature of the hero and in the fact that the novel, including early versions and late fragments, was a life's work covering the period 1898 to 1942. It appears equally evident that Nietzsche, and not similarly oriented thinkers in whom Musil was simultaneously absorbed, was the principal inspiration for the ideas discussed above. Admittedly, Musil had read Emerson and been impressed by him. On occasion he linked the names of Emerson and Nietzsche. In one diary reference, for example, he acknowledges his debt to the two men: "Es gibt Augenblicke großer Wahrhaftigkeit, wo ich mir eingestehe, alles, was ich sage, habe viel besser schon Emerson oder Nietzsche gesagt. Ich werde nicht nur davon überwältigt, wenn ich solche Stellen wieder sehe, sondern ich muß auch annehmen, daß ein tatsächlicher Einfluß im Spiel ist" (III, 706). Musil juxtaposed the names of the two men again in a commentary to a diagram stressing the importance of the "andern Zustand": "Unserer Zeit das Problem von Emerson vermacht, schließlich auch durch Nietzsche. Sie hat es nicht gelöst, sondern gespalten in Rationalismus und Religion" (*KW*, 299).

When one reflects, however, on the areas in which Emerson and Nietzsche held similar views, it becomes obvious that a rather clear line of demarcation can be drawn between them, as Emerson remained at all times a transcendental idealist.[15] Thus, the inner voice which guided Emerson's heroic genius was no will to power but *ein frommes Empfangen*. And whereas his superman was no weakling and not easily swayed, still he was not permitted to disregard his neighbor's rights completely.

[15] Stanley Hubbard, *Nietzsche und Emerson* (Basel, 1958), p. 196. Musil, himself, believed the similarity between Nietzsche and Emerson to be superficial: "Denn diese beiden sind trotz mancher Verwandtschaft zu unähnlich" (III, 706).

The Impact of Nietzsche on Hermann Hesse

In his short autobiographical novel, *Nuremberg Journey* (*Die Nürnberger Reise*) written in 1927, Hesse mentions an evening stroll in the old part of Tuttlingen, a town in Swabia. The romantic atmosphere awakened memories of his youthful enthusiasm for Hölderlin's poem "Die Nacht" and of his equally strong enthusiasm in later years for *Thus Spake Zarathustra*:

> Never again, although I had read much and enthusiastically in my youth, did the words of a poet fascinate me as completely as did these words the young boy. And later, when at twenty I read in Zarathustra for the first time and was similarly fascinated, the Hölderlin poem in the reader and that first astonishment of my boyish soul in the presence of art came to mind once again.[1]

Nietzsche must indeed have been an overpowering experience for the twenty-year old Hesse. The short essay "On Moving into a New House" ("Beim Einzug in ein neues Haus," 1931) reveals that at twenty Hesse, although in dire financial straits, had purchased two expensive portraits of the philosopher. Especially the picture of Nietzsche taken during his illness "with completely sunken and distant gaze" made a strong impression on him (IV, 615).

In the same essay, still ruminating on his youth, Hesse alludes to his "intoxicated, even frenzied absorption first with Goethe and then with Nietzsche," and to the dominant role played by Nietzsche during his [Hesse's] stay in Basel:

> The small circle of friends in Basel that took me in and helped educate me was completely under the influence of Jacob Burckhardt, who had died

---

[1] Hermann Hesse, *Gesammelte Schriften* (Frankfurt am Main: Suhrkamp Verlag, 1958) IV, 148. All further references to Hesse's work will be to this edition; volume and page number will be given in the body of the text. The English translations in this essay have been made by the present writer.

only recently and who, in the second half of my life, came gradually to fill the place that had previously belonged to Nietzsche. (IV, 616)

Goethe dominated the early years and Burckhardt the later ones, but in the interim Hesse had been especially attracted to Nietzsche. The lines quoted would indicate that Nietzsche was the strongest influence during this "interim," which on closer examination may be seen to encompass the major portion of his creative existence (1899–1930).[2] Memoirs Hesse penned in 1951 describing his arrival in Basel confirm this opinion; he confides how "enthusiastic for Nietzsche" he was at the time and adds that although he cherished Basel "above all (as) the city of Nietzsche, Jacob Burckhardt and Böcklin," Nietzsche had at first completely overshadowed Burckhardt:

> Even then I had been reading him [Burckhardt]. I had read his *Culture of the Renaissance* in Tübingen and his *Constantine* in Basel, but I was still too enthralled with Nietzsche to be fully receptive to his [Burckhardt's] ideas.[3]

Another significant revelation as to the importance of Nietzsche for Hesse's life and work is to be found in Hesse's masterpiece and final dictum of 1943, *Magister Ludi* (*Glasperlenspiel*). It will be shown subsequently that Pater Jakobus and the brilliant but unreliable glassbead-player Tegularius are transparent disguises for Burckhardt and Nietzsche. The fictional narrator says of the autobiographical hero, Josef Knecht:

> It is our opinion that Tegularius was as necessary and important in shaping Knecht's life as were Designori and the Pater in Marienfels, and indeed in the same manner as they, as an inspirational force, as an open window to new viewpoints. (VI, 367)

Inasmuch as the character Designori was a practical man of the world who merely reinforced the historical and institutional views of Burckhardt, it is evident that here again Burckhardt and Nietzsche are pitted against one another as the two most significant inspirational forces which helped to form Hesse's outlook.

[2] It may appear strange that Hesse would consider the period beginning only a year or so before the time of writing as the "second half" of his life, when he was already 54 years of age. It must not be forgotten, however, that Hesse's marriage to Ninon Ausländer brought him such happiness that he viewed life from then on as a new beginning. The terminating date of Hesse's Nietzsche-period will be considered in detail below.

[3] "Ein paar Basler Erinnerungen," *Die Weltwoche* (Zurich, 22 March 1951), p. 17.

These statements are admissions by Hesse of his debt to Nietzsche. They carry particular weight when one recalls that Hesse never tried to create a legend about himself and was in all such matters scrupulously honest and painfully self-analytical. And these admissions can be reinforced by additional comments which reveal Hesse's continued interest in and admiration for Nietzsche.

In 1918, for example, Hesse praised certain writings by Freud, Jung, Stekel and other psychologists, in part because these writings affirmed and improved Nietzsche's findings (VII, 138). The following year he expressed astonishment that Dostoevski should attract German youth more than Goethe "or even Nietzsche" (VII, 162), and he recommended that a correspondent take another look at the last pages of the second *Thought out of Season* (*Unzeitgemäße Betrachtung*), so that he might recognize the difficult task facing "youth destined to strangle a moribund pseudo-culture and then to begin anew" (VII, 234). At about the same time Hesse came to the conclusion in "Sampling of Books" ("Bücherprobe") that Nietzsche was "essential, including the correspondence" (VII, 187). In 1921 Hesse expressed admiration for the prose music of *Zarathustra* (VII, 252) and six years later for the style of *Ecce Homo* which he felt was a desperate attempt to achieve the reconciliation between art and truth demanded by his generation (IV, 157). "The Magic of Life" ("Magie des Lebens," 1930) terms Nietzsche the long misunderstood genius who prepared the way for at least "several dozen thinkers" (VII, 349–50). An essay on Goethe written in 1932 stresses by indirection the importance of the Nietzsche experience: ". . . no other writer except Nietzsche ever engrossed, attracted, tormented me to the same degree, forced me to reflect to the same degree" (VII, 376). A few pages further on Hesse refers both to the duration and depth of this experience: "Many a year I plagued myself with Goethe and let him become the disturbing element in my spiritual life, him and Nietzsche" (VII, 378). "A Night at Work" ("Eine Arbeitsnacht," 1928), views the dreams and hopes of the poet-philosopher Nietzsche as an important contribution to both German and European culture (VII, 305), and a letter written in 1934 includes him in the community of great suffering and creative spirits (VII, 565). The eulogy for Christian Schrempf (1944) "defends . . . the pathologic personality" as such and in particular "Nietzsche, who was at that time revered by me," against the moralistic attacks of the eccentric theologian (IV, 770–77). Similarly, the essay, "Concerning Good and Bad Critics" written over a decade earlier (1930), discussed how difficult it was for intelligent and gifted people to live in our times. Once people recognized this difficulty, "Hölderlin and Nietzsche would be converted back from psychopaths to geniuses" (VII, 369). In his last published reference to Nietzsche (1953), Hesse relates how excited it still made him to view the house in Sils Maria where Nietzsche had lived. Clinging defiantly to the rugged mountain-side, it "awakened respect and pity and served as an urgent reminder of the noble human ideal which the hermit even in his erroneous teachings had posed" (VII, 849–50).

★   ★   ★

Before considering Hesse's principal works in chronological order, it will be well to enumerate briefly the main themes in Hesse's writing that reveal a spiritual affinity to Nietzsche:

1. The present-day bourgeois world is decadent and must be revitalized.
2. Such revitalization can only be brought about through the deeds of the really great individuals, of the geniuses.
3. The genius is a person with a strong sense of mission. The purpose of his life is to understand his inner voice and to obey it.
4. Whatever the inner voice commands should be done in a courageous and joyous manner. (Nietzsche's *amor fati* is here merged with the pietistic *Unio mystica*).
5. It is normal and justified for a sensitive (inspired) person to react pathologically to present-day decadence. (Hesse himself attests to the frequency of this theme in his works [IV, 58]).
6. A rather weak, pathologic individual with traits of the genius is confronted by a strong, intelligent, merciless, artistic superman. Sometimes the two are different sides of the same person, sometimes the superman is initially an independent entity and yet is ultimately identified as an aspect of the protagonist, and then again he is occasionally portrayed as an entirely independent personality.
7. The world-structure vacillates between chaos and divine order. In the course of each novel, chaos is overcome. Hesse's heroes ultimately come to believe in a divine essence located in the heart of man. This insight is reached, however, *in every case* only after a long and bitter battle with nihilism.

The early poems, *Romantic Songs* (*Romantische Lieder*, 1897) and the nine prose studies, *An Hour beyond Midnight* (*Eine Stunde hinter Mitternacht*) reveal essentially an attitude of romantic pessimism. Hence our investigation will begin by considering the first of Hesse's many autobiographical novels, *The Posthumous Writings and Poems of Hermann Lauscher* (*Die hinterlassenen Schriften und Gedichte von Hermann Lauscher*, 1901), which was conceived in part while Hesse was still in Tübingen. In this novel the main link to Nietzsche is found in the character of the hero and his disdain for bourgeois life. Although Lauscher in some ways resembles an enamored Werther, he is more the strong, moody, outsider-artist, who refuses to create because he believes the world bereft of meaning.

Lauscher views the world from a dionysion-apollonian perspective. To his way of thinking the drives of the subconscious resemble a subterranean world which, when suddenly released, surge upward to mock and crush "his white temples and favorite illusions." He leaves unanswered the question as to whether he believes in Christ. Instead he directs his entire attention to an aesthetic religion that measures all spiritual and material things in terms of their relationship to beauty. In this regard one thinks of Novalis whom Hesse revered. But one thinks also of Nietzsche who saw the world justified only as a work of art. Hesse's friend and biographer, Hugo Ball, thought he detected Nietzschean influence in the frequent shifts in mood on the part of the hero from romantic intoxication to cynical sobriety.

Hesse's first successful novel *Peter Camenzind* (1904) evaluates the Nietzschean ethic but then rejects it; the altruism of St. Francis of Assisi triumphs over the immoralism of Zarathustra. After many educational experiences including a sojourn in Assisi, Camenzind concludes that his adherence to the master-morality had not been justified:

> Formerly, without ever actually having prayed to Zarathustra, I had been a master-type (*Herrenmensch*) and had neglected neither my self-veneration nor my disdain for simpler people. Now I saw with increasing clarity that there were no firm boundaries, and that for the little people, the oppressed and the poor, life was not only just as complex, but usually warmer, truer and more exemplary than for the favored and illustrious. (I, 325)

Despite this rejection of the master-morality—by no means final as Hesse's contempt for mediocrity caused his love of humanity to waver time and again—, Nietzsche's impact on the novel is note-worthy. Camenzind is another Lauscher, a strong yet sensitive artist-type whose doctor urges him to give up his inner isolation if he does not want "to lose his mental equilibrium." His abhorrence of bourgeois culture induces him to sacrifice a promising career as a writer. Like Lauscher, he oscillates between romantic moods and a cynical intellectualism. When he is stimulated by his beloved red wine, he turns into a ruthless critic who attacks the decadence of the times with Nietzschean severity.

At the university only the ideas of Nietzsche and St. Francis impress the young Camenzind. Nietzsche's importance for the novel and its hero is highlighted in the scene in which the youth first learns of the philosopher. When he admits ignorance to his friend Richard, the latter cries out in amazement, "Nietzsche. Why, great heavens, you mean you don't know about him?" and was thoroughly delighted at Camenzind's naiveté (I, 259).

The novel *Under the Wheel* (*Unterm Rad*, 1905) tells the tragic story of a gifted student who is overtaxed and ultimately destroyed by his pedantic teachers. The young protagonist Hans Giebenrath, when first introduced to the reader, is viewed as a product of decadence in a Nietzschean frame of reference:

> Recalling the weakness of the mother and the considerable age of the family, a sensitive observer schooled in the modern manner might have spoken of hypertrophy of the intelligence as a symptom of incipient decadence. (I, 376)

The link with Nietzsche is especially clear from the next lines:

> But the city was fortunate in not having any people of this sort . . . one could still live there and be cultured without being familiar with the speeches of Zarathustra. (I, 376–77)

With fine irony Hesse lets it be understood that in this smug little town, which neither knew nor cared to know anything about Nietzsche's modern ideas, there was little likelihood of encountering sympathy or understanding for the problem of decadence.

Another Nietzschean aspect of the novel is its fundamental concern with the exceptional person, the artistic superman, the genius. To be sure, only Giebenrath's friend, Hermann Heilner, is portrayed as a real genius. But it is said of young Hans that "the mysterious spark from above [of inspiration] had indeed fallen for once into the old hamlet" (I, 376). Spark, fire, mission, these are all designations by means of which Hesse refers to the inspiration of genius. Thus, Hans, too, is an incipient genius. The inner congruence of the two lads is emphasized by their close friendship.[4]

Heilner represents an ideal rather than reality and is clearly Nietzschean, though it is interesting to note that in some respects he bears more resemblance to an idealized Nietzsche than to the artistic superman. Robust, "at times wild and almost cruel" (I, 437) and a loner, Heilner abhors both the petty diligence of his fellow students and the pedantry of his teachers. He is artistic—like Camenzind and Lauscher he is a gifted writer with a satiric bent. Like them he is inclined to melancholy (I, 443) and (like Nietzsche!) exposed to attacks of moodiness when the weather was bad (I, 450). As with all true geniuses, however, "this pathologic melancholia was only the freeing of superfluous and unhealthy impulses" (I, 451).

Giebenrath does not fit the pattern of the superman as well; although he possesses the spark of genius, he does not have the strength to withstand the destructive impact of the boarding school. His divergence from the pattern results from the fact that he represents the real, the author himself, to a degree modern man in his helplessness, and the tortuous road which Giebenrath must follow through all the phases of neurosis to his ultimate destruction is one Hesse was to describe many times more as the road he believed modern man, too, had to go.

The nihilistic undercurrent in the novel is only partially vitiated by a vague *amor fati*. It is said of Heilner that "after many further genial pranks and aberrations he mastered the suffering of life."

Nihilism continued to remain an important factor in Hesse's thinking, as may be seen in the sad tale, *The Marble Saw* (*Die Marmorsäge*, 1908). Here the romantic hero is confronted by the learned and skeptical farm-superintendent, Gustav Becker, who destroys his optimistic principles:

> Frequently without the use of any words and merely by a horribly expressive grin, he made me doubt my own statements about life and mankind, and sometimes he even ventured to say that every kind of worldly wisdom was ridiculous. (I, 558)

Becker's nihilistic view is confirmed not only by the tragic outcome of the narrative but also by the early realization of the hero that his optimism

---

[4] The contrast of ideal and real, ego and anima, which in the case of Lauscher and Camenzind was still encompassed in one person, will henceforth frequently be projected by Hesse in two distinct individuals.

resembled "the happiness of the fairy prince" which he knew "never lasts very long" (I, 552).

Nihilism is a motif in *Walter Kömpff*, another story by Hesse, also written in 1908. Driven to desperation, Kömpff goes mad and concludes with Nietzsche: "This dear God you speak of. He is nowhere, he doesn't exist" (II, 258). The author makes it clear that he is not to be identified with the insane protagonist, yet he ends the story with these revealing words: "And few people gave any thought to the matter of how close we all live to the darkness, in the shades of which Walter Kömpff went astray" (II, 259).

But nihilism was never more than a component in Hesse's thought and his feelings continued to waver between nihilism and *amor fati*, just as Nietzsche's had done. In some of the other stories of this period, *amor fati*, the idea of a life-affirming compulsion, takes thematic precedence over nihilism, although frequently the inner drive has aspects of a Christian conscience. The theme in *Emil Kolb* is the protagonist's inability "to hear the call of nature within himself" (II, 395). This lack of inner consistency leaves him exposed to the vicissitudes of fortune; a "passing mood" (II, 412) leads him to petty theft and ultimate ruin (II, 429). Ladidel's "purity of heart" (II, 262) smacks more of Luther than Nietzsche, as it implies a meek Christian acceptance of destiny; when Ladidel realizes that he does not have the makings of a notary, he willingly—and with the author's full approval—accepts the modest career of a barber (II, 304).

In the story *Hay-Moon (Heumond)*, however, *amor fati* has a more Nietzschean ring. The pedantic tutor Homburger lacks, like Kolb, "a commanding and inviolable essence" (I, 685). He is consequently portrayed as a shallow idealist who reads his heroes Nietzsche and Ruskin only in watered-down popularizations as he would be unable to grasp their significance in the original (I, 685); that is to say, he lacks the inner drive and hence cannot understand Nietzsche's message of *amor fati*. Homburger's words ring hollow when he pompously asserts that only geniuses can alter the course of history (I, 694). Young Peter Abderegg on the other hand represents the ideal as he has inner strength and the courage of his convictions.

The conflict of nihilism and *amor fati* is the principal theme in the novel *Gertrud*, written in 1910. Here the main characters, the crippled composer Kuhn and the strong and handsome singer Muoth, are both beset by the problems of nihilism. In contrast to *Under the Wheel*, however, the strong artist succumbs, whereas the weak composer Kuhn manages through his art to come to limited terms with life.

The predominantly nihilistic tone of the novel is symbolized by its leitmotif, Nietzsche's lament, "God is dead." This outcry occurs in a poem Kuhn had set to music. The last strophe reads:

> Does he not see me hovering
> In mortal anguish and suffering?
> Alas, God is dead!
> —And I should continue to live? (II, 40)

It was this poem that led to Kuhn's friendship with Muoth; the latter immediately sensed that even if Kuhn had not written the words, he "must have experienced them" (II, 40). Nihilism was the common bond.

Muoth's nihilistic conviction is reinforced by an unhappy marriage and he commits suicide. To the bitter end he holds to the belief: "I believe as did Buddha that life has no value" (II, 188).

Kuhn also finds "everything false and stupid" (II, 127) and even at the end of the novel he still views the world as cruel and meaningless: "Destiny was not good. Life was fickle and cruel. There was to be found in nature neither goodness nor reason" (II, 191). In the period of his greatest tribulation, Kuhn is informed by his former teacher, Lotze, that he is a pathologic case:

> You suffer from a malady which unfortunately is fashionable and which one encounters daily in intelligent individuals. Doctors naturally know nothing about it. This ailment is related to *moral insanity* and can also be termed individualism or imagined loneliness . . . It happens that at times such sick people become arrogant and condemn other people, who are healthy and can still understand and love one another, as the common herd (*Herdenvieh*). Were this sickness to become universal, humanity would die out. But it occurs only in Central Europe and there only in the upper classes. (II, 128)

It is apparent that the "moral insanity"[5] of which Lotze speaks is closely related to Nietzsche's immoralism. Consequently, when Lotze suggests that Kuhn's cure can only be effected if he were to concern himself more with helping other people, it is clear that the basic duality, St. Francis contra Nietzsche, is again in evidence. However, for a time Kuhn rejects the doctrine of unselfish love taught by St. Francis, as he finds that even with the best of intentions he cannot really help his aged mother or alter her situation.

[5] Hesse wrote "moral insanity" in English.

Ultimately Kuhn struggles through to *amor fati*, to a life-view that affirms life despite its pain. He reaches the conclusion that if one affirms pain, in time one can scarcely differentiate it from happiness (II, 34). He comes to believe that goodness and reason exist in man, although nature and destiny remain cruel and coincidental (II, 191). Through art Kuhn reestablishes his faith in God; in rare creative moments "when the dark depths are silent" he feels "the divine within himself" (II, 191). The ultimate *Unio mystica* reached by Kuhn is of course quite un-Nietzschean. But Kuhn's stress on nihilism and pain prior to the achievement of his transitory affirmation, reveals the extent to which Nietzsche's concept of *amor fati* lay imbedded in Hesse's thinking.

In its manifold use of archetypal symbolism, dream analysis and introspection, *Demian* (1917) is structurally indebted to the psychoanalytic theories of Carl Jung; the ethical ideas expressed in the novel, however, are a reformulation of Nietzsche's views.

Once again the leitmotif has been unmistakably selected in the spirit of the great immoralist; it is the sign of Cain. With Nietzschean irony and emphasis on the "bad," Hesse chose the first murderer, the first villain in world history to serve as his model of a truly great man. In a letter dated 1930 Hesse writes:

> And so it seems to me that Cain, the outlawed criminal, the first murderer, may very easily be interpreted as a defamed Prometheus, as a representative of the intellect and of freedom, who was punished with banishment for his curiosity and daring. (VII, 488)

In the novel the hero is permitted to express a similar opinion. The stalwart Demian tells his weaker friend Sinclair the story of Cain from the Nietzschean viewpoint. As Demian[6] sees it, the conventional version was in all likelihood a crass lie invented by the weak to slander this strong and dreaded outsider (III, 125–26).

Thus Cain is viewed as a promethean individual, an outsider, a superman, and his sign thus becomes the symbol of the chosen few. The importance of the Cain leitmotif in the novel may be seen from the fact that it reappears at every significant moment in Sinclair's life: during the religious instruction prior to his confirmation (III, 148), during his initiation into the dark world of the senses (III, 165), and at the moment of self-realization

---

[6] In numerous ways, Hesse makes it clear that Demian is to be understood as the artistic projection of Sinclair's *anima* or ideal.

when, on meeting Frau Eva, he is aware that he bears the sign on his own forehead (III, 236). In Sinclair's last vision the God-Mother appears, resembling Frau Eva, a giantess, stars in her hair, with the sign of Cain upon her brow (III, 255). Thus the sign of Cain accompanies the hero from his first uncertain steps into life to his final comprehensive vision.

As is evident from his use of the Cain leitmotif, Hesse was concerned in the novel with proclaiming a new morality beyond conventional good and evil. Seeking to encourage the dispirited soldiers of the defeated German army, he implied that the new morality was for "everyone," but actually his interest, as always, was directed toward the strong individuals imbued with a sense of mission. He conceived these strong individuals in the manner of Nietzschean supermen, as a closer inspection of Demian shows.

The mysterious Demian is without flaw; he is reserved, courageous, strong, intelligent, filled with a sense of destiny. He divides mankind into leaders and the "herd" (III, 228). As shown above, he attributes customary morality to the resentment of the weak, who seek through cunning to force their slave morality upon the strong. With Nietzsche, he prefers the pale thief who when crucified with Christ refused to repent (III, 155). Although not a drinker, Demian recognized the dionysiac power of alcohol to awaken heightened states of mind, which he refers to approvingly as "intoxicated" and "bacchic" (III, 180). He prefers the life of an intoxicated individual to that of the "virtuous citizen" because the former is "presumably more vital" (III, 180). He loathes modern European culture with its "country fair of technology and science" (III, 229), and in consonance with Nietzsche's conception of cultural decadence, he predicts the passing of western civilization (III, 228). He is convinced that the salvation of mankind lies in the hands of the select few who bear the sign of Cain and who are predestined to shake the philistines from their heavy slumber. Demian reveres the principle of *amor fati* more strongly even than Kuhn, although he knows that the path leads without fail to the tragic loneliness and desperation of Jesus in the Garden of Gethsemane (III, 222). The strength of his conviction is attributed to his belief that man's destiny lies completely within himself. Demian's inner voice resembles the "bow of longing" and the "will to power" of Nietzsche's creative superman, to the extent that neither Hesse nor Nietzsche was concerned with outer destiny or superficial gratification of the ego. But whereas Nietzsche virtually identified the inner command with the self, Hesse stressed once again that the inner voice was the manifestation of a higher power. Young Sinclair makes this clear when he recognizes the meaning of destiny for the first time:

And here suddenly the knowledge burned me like a searing flame:—there was an "office" for each individual, but not one that he might select, delimit and administer at will . . . the true mission for each individual was simply this: to find himself. He might end up as a poet or as a demented individual, as a prophet or as a criminal—that was not his concern, indeed in the final analysis that was unimportant. It was his business to find his own destiny, not just any destiny, and to live this destiny to the full, completely and unbroken. . . . I was a toss of nature, a toss into the unknown, perhaps towards something new, perhaps towards nothing, and to permit this toss to fulfill itself, to feel its will in me and make it completely a part of me, that alone was my destiny. (III, 220–21)

Demian's belief that the inner voice is a reflection of Nature induces him to subordinate his activist tendency to reform the world in favor of a kind of religious passivity. Despite his violent opposition to the philistines with their "will to endure," (III, 238), he insists that he and his compatriots will take no initiative but will await the inner command of destiny. The robust Demian and the cripple Kuhn are in terms of outlook not so far apart as it might seem. But whereas for Kuhn *amor fati* was a step to the achievement of the pietistic *unio mystica*, Demian and his friend Sinclair fuse the two concepts.

The mystical affirmation in *Demian* might lead one to believe that there was little room in the novel for the ugly specter of nihilism. One must not forget, however, that at the time of writing the author was experiencing the most difficult years of his life. Branded a traitor to his country, his wife mentally ill, Hesse was so close to despair that he put himself in the care of a psychiatrist. Indeed, if one disregards for a brief moment the dazzling goal of the hero, it becomes readily apparent that as with Hesse's previous novels, many pages in *Demian* are concerned with the inner uncertainty of the tormented protagonist.

Hesse, himself, was quite ready to admit that the ideals he posited in his novels remained ideals, and that his "confessions of unusual and, so-to-speak, ideal experiences" alternated with "confessions of inadequacy, weakness, hellish torment and desperation" (VII, 509). Moments of positive faith were followed by moments of insecurity and pessimism: "That my positive and my negative side, my strength and my weakness can only be expressed chronologically in an alternation between bright and dark, is something that I cannot change" (VII, 509).

A meaningful sign that Hesse was still plagued with doubt and still exposed to the threat of nihilism when he wrote *Demian* may be seen in the generally conceded fact that in these years he engrossed himself in Nietzsche's ideas. A careful reading makes clear that *Demian* represents not so much an acceptance of, as a debate with Nietzsche, the spokesman of the superman and *amor fati*, to be sure, but also the spokesman of nihilism. In *Demian* Hesse sought to come to grips with Nietzsche; specifically, he sought to overcome nihilism and to integrate the superman into an absolute world order.

When one considers the manner in which God is presented in *Demian*, one notes a similar attempt to reconcile Nietzschean and Christian views. Hesse affirms the Nietzschean preeminence of the instincts but exalts these to mythical stature in the figure of the God-Mother. How closely the dark mother world was associated with Nietzsche in Hesse's thinking may be gleaned from the fact that the God-Mother Eva disappeared from his writings when he finally rejected Nietzsche's ideas completely in the early 1930's. The synthesis of Nietzschean and Christian outlooks is suggested in Sinclair's ability to regard Frau Eva as "mother, beloved, goddess" (III, 233). Over a decade later Hesse has Goldmund refer to Frau Eva with almost identical words, "mother, madonna and beloved" (V, 65). The God-Mother awakens both sensual and spiritual love, she encompasses not only the dark sinful world of the mother but also the bright virtuous (Christian) world of the father.

Before leaving this discussion of *Demian*, it should be pointed out that Sinclair himself twice refers to Nietzsche as an important factor in his own development. On reading Novalis, Sinclair notes that seldom had an author so impressed him "except perhaps Nietzsche" (III, 178). Then at the university, although generally disappointed by his philosophical studies, he was delighted with his readings in Nietzsche:

> I lived with him, felt the solitude of his soul, sensed the destiny that drove him inevitably onward, suffered with him and was blissful, that there had been such a person, who went his own way so resolutely. (III, 225)

Demian also refers to Nietzsche. Speaking of great individuals filled with a sense of destiny, he cites Jesus and Nietzsche: "What nature wants from an individual, stands written in that individual, in you and in me. It was written in Jesus, it was written in Nietzsche" (III, 229).

The pietistically flavored *amor fati* of *Demian* also provides the core of two essays written in 1919, both of which reveal Nietzschean inspiration. The first of these bears the title "Eigensinn"[7] and begins in the pseudo-

---

[7] Hesse plays with the word *Eigensinn* using it both in its usual sense of "stubbornness" and "obstinacy," and its literal meaning of "sense of self," "self-awareness." Thus *Eigensinn* catches the full flavor of the egotistical Nietzschean morality.

biblical style of *Thus Spake Zarathustra*: "Eine Tugend gibt es, die liebe ich sehr, eine einzige. Sie heißt Eigensinn" (There is one virtue that I love dearly. It is called *Eigensinn*; VII, 194). The stylistic innuendo is appropriate as the essay attacks bourgeois morality and berates its virtues as little more than different forms of obedience. The second and longer essay, "Zarathustra's Return" ("Zarathustras Wiederkehr") imitates the Zarathustra-style throughout, admittedly as a means to attract the attention of German youth. The skill with which Hesse both recaptured the style and reproduced Nietzsche's arguments, while yet modifying them, shows his close familiarity with Nietzsche's masterpiece. The smiling sage Zarathustra "who has seen much and who no longer has sympathy with tears" (one thinks of Hesse's characters—Vasudeva, Buddha, the Music Master—III, 201) praises the self-love (*Eigenliebe*) of his disciples. He also lauds solitude and suffering as a means of strengthening man and leading him to a realization of the necessity to accept destiny (VII, 206). Then, however, shifting to Hesse's own line of reasoning Zarathustra asserts, "Whoever has recognized destiny will never seek to change destiny" (VII, 207) and mocks the young soldiers who had hoped through their suffering to change the course of the world (VII, 213). Zarathustra's farewell address is reminiscent of Sinclair's words at the moment of realization: "In each of you there is a call, a will, a toss of nature, a toss into the future, towards the new and the higher— there is no God other than dwells within you" (VII, 229).

The three stories contained in the collection *Klingsor's Last Summer* (*Klingsors Letzter Sommer*) contain numerous Nietzschean motifs. All three have as their basic theme existential fear and the need to affirm destiny.

"A Child's Soul" ("Kinderseele") treats the question of whether the dark urgings of a child toward the bad are not just as much a call of destiny as is the love of order derived from the bright father-world. The author reveals his bias by introducing Nietzsche's "noble criminal" into the story. The latter is no petty, fearful thief but a proud fellow, pale and smiling, who holds his head high while being led along by his guards. The scolding citizenry accompanying him are scornfully referred to as "rabble" (*Pack und Pöbel*, III, 444), and it is clear that this man is to be regarded as a second Cain, as a person who heeds his inner voice. Although destiny has brought him into conflict with bourgeois justice, he does not let this disturb his inner calm, for he understands and accepts life.

In the story "Klein and Wagner," one encounters pathologic rejection of the bourgeois way of life, the notion of justifiable homicide and disdain for Richard Wagner. Once again the theme is *amor fati* with new shades of meaning. The bank-teller Klein has embezzled funds so that he may flee bourgeois hypocrisy and lead a meaningful existence. He is attracted to a beautiful dancer who obeys only her inner law. When Teresina dances, she is "like a tree or a mountain or an animal or a star, existing solely for herself—regardless of whether this be good or bad" (III, 510).

But things go awry. Klein has misunderstood himself and realizes belatedly that the trouble lay not in middle-class morality but in his own sexual impotence and fear of life. He finds no other recourse than to take his life by drowning and does so. At the moment, however, when he "lets himself go," when he wills with his whole heart not to will, he suddenly realizes that life can be affirmed. Such detachment and abnegation are not contrary to pietism, but the setting and vocabulary indicate additionally the influence of Schopenhauer.[8] Furthermore, Klein's affirmation, in which the world regains its beauty and every woman becomes desirable if not necessary, suggests the affirming-negating Hindu Yoga.

In the title story, the orgiastic artist Klingsor has an intense fear of death. Although not prepared to accept the mystical solution of his magician friend—Schopenhauer's repudiation of time—he summons the courage to face reality. Whereupon he draws a self-portrait which reveals his very soul:

> It is man, *ecce homo*, the tired, greedy, wild, childlike and sophisticated man of our late era, the dying European, anxious to die . . . filled with smouldering passion and at the same time totally exhausted, resigned to destiny and to pain. (III, 610)

Recognizing his tragic destiny, Klingsor goes his way, having regained his inner peace.

The pathologic Klingsor resembles not only the author in his distress, but also in large measure Nietzsche. It may well be that Hesse in his depression feared that he would suffer a fate similar to Nietzsche's.

Numerous parallels link Klingsor with Nietzsche. The artist's last period of hectic creativity bears a strong resemblance to the comparable period of tremendous productivity in Nietzsche's life shortly before he went mad. The self-portrait of the artist, "his gigantic confession," provides a striking counterpart to the penetrating self-analysis Nietzsche attempted

---

[8] It would appear more than chance that the last scene in the story parallels closely Schopenhauer's famous description of man who, in the face of chaos, relies on the principal of individuation, like a boatman who trusts his tiny boat in a threatening sea. Hesse writes, "Sein kleines Boot, das war er, das war sein kleines, umgrenztes, künstlich versichertes Leben—rundum aber das weite Grau, das war die Welt, das war All und Gott . . ." (III, 548).

in *Ecce Homo* at the very end of his sane existence. It is probably no chance coincidence that hostile critics referred to *Ecce Homo* in the same way that critics spoke of Klingsor's self-portrait, as an indication of "apparent insanity" (III, 609). Like his apparent model, Klingsor experienced a final euphoria, living the last days "like one who is ecstatic" (III, 611) and calming his nerves with veronal.

With the publication of *Siddhartha* (1919–1922) Hesse had recovered his composure and was able to express in quieter fashion the outlook contained in "Klein and Wagner." This *amor fati*, which synthesizes the thoughts of Nietzsche and Schopenhauer with Hindu Yoga and the mystical pantheism of St. Francis, may be said to represent the fundamental belief, the mystical ideal, of the mature author. It is of course true that Sinclair and Camenzind had a somewhat similar outlook. But as Hesse admitted in *Resort Guest* (*Kurgast*, 1925), the ideal of his maturity was nothing new; although his thoughts had changed slightly in the course of twenty years, his hopes and dreams had remained the same (IV, 104).

After initial failures—experiments in ascetic and sensualistic ways of living—Siddhartha triumphs over his ego. He does this in the same way that Klein had done, by negating the will in an attempt to drown himself. At the crucial moment, however, when he discovers that the complete negation of life can lead to its affirmation, he decides to continue living. But his education is not yet finished. He must stand a still further test. He must experience the bitter pain of an anguished parent before he can discover the full importance of love:

> Love, O Govinda, appears to me to be of prime importance. . . . The only thing that now matters to me is to be able to love the world, not to disdain it, not to hate it and myself, but to be able to observe it and myself and all beings with love and admiration and respect. (III, 729)

Only now can his sense of totality reach its full culmination, can the river teach him of the timeless perfection of the world. Only now "did Siddhartha cease to struggle with destiny, cease to suffer . . ." (III, 721).

The leitmotif in the novel and the symbol of *amor fati* is the bird whose voice transmits the inner commands to the strong and handsome Siddhartha. When the unfortunate hero strays from his path, he dreams the bird has died and its voice remains silent. But he hears the bird's voice anew when, after negating the will, he is again able to affirm the world and achieve a new sense of totality.

In the novel *Resort Guest* the hero becomes so enraged at the superficial way of life in a small health resort that he temporarily loses faith in his sense of mission. But laughter makes it possible for him to reconcile himself with the inevitable (IV, 94), and nature with its immanent *Eigensinn* offers him renewed proof of the inner unity of the world (IV, 53, 102). Once again he is prepared to speak of love (IV, 110), once again ready to obey the "dark commands" within him, once again he will strive to fuse the antithetical poles of his existence (IV, 115).

Nature is here symbolized by two caged martins. Without being inconsistent, these animals are simple and lovable and at the same time wild and cruel. Curious and trusting as children, they nevertheless exude "the wild, pungent odor of a beast of prey" (IV, 53). In nature there is no hypocrisy; the animals remain true to themselves and follow their inner law.

In *Resort Guest* Hesse's abhorrence for the bourgeois world includes even the realm of the intellect, a direction which was already indicated in *Siddhartha*. The enraged resort guest levels his entire wrath at a pedantic bourgeois patient:

> You exist, I should like to say, on the level of paper, of money and credit, of morality, of law, of intellect, of respectability. You are a space-and-time contemporary (*Raum- und Zeitgenosse*) imbued with virtue, the categorical imperative, and reason, and perhaps you are even related to the thing-in-itself and to capitalism. But you don't possess the element of reality that I find in every stone and tree. (IV, 98)

The two references to Nietzsche in the novel indicate that the psychological and sociological viewpoints presented there are at least in part attributable to him. The resort guest says that he has derived his theory of neurosis from Nietzsche and Hamsun. This admission is pertinent as the novel is the supposed diary of a neurotic. Nietzsche's name is also mentioned in connection with Hesse's ultra-personal problem as to whether a pathologic attitude is justified in our time. The resort guest decides not to discuss this question which he considers the basic problem "of all sensitive intellectuals since Nietzsche," since it has been the main theme in almost all of his earlier writing (IV, 58).

Resort Guest rejected the intellect and found unity in nature. At first glance, *Steppenwolf* (1927) would seem to demonstrate a diametrically opposed point of view, as in this famous novel the earlier innocence and unity of nature is declared to be a myth. We are told that the way does not lead back to nature and to early childhood, but onward to ever greater guilt and humanity: not back from duality to unity, but on to endless dichotomies and to the gradual assumption of the entire universe in one's soul. The objective, however, remains the same as before: "return into the All, elimination of painful individuation, divinification" (IV, 249–50).

Although it is no longer possible to return to unity in nature, this does not preclude pushing forward along the road to consecrated sensuality; the dark mother-world of instinct is not banned from the scene. We learn that a man with an inner calling can achieve his aim just as fully by becoming a sensualist as by becoming a saint. Had the hero of the novel, Harry Haller, pursued either of these routes with sufficient persistence, he would have achieved the absolute:

> We see that he had within him a strong impulse not only toward the saint but also toward the sensualist. Because of some weakness or lethargy, however, he could not manage the leap into the free, wild space of the Absolute. (IV, 238–39)

In any case, Hesse considers the duality of nature and spirit as an artistic simplification by means of which he can represent the infinite possibilities of the human soul (IV, 243). So that we do not misunderstand his "wolf's theory," he tells us the wolf also includes the bird of paradise (IV, 251). The Nietzschean world of instinct is still complete.

Not only the metaphysical underpinnings but also the plot of this novel makes use of Nietzschean ideas. Thus the polarity burgher versus outsider is obviously borrowed from the Nietzschean antithesis of herd and master. The burgher is viewed as a weakling who prefers the rule of the "herd" (IV, 237), so that he himself need not assume power and responsibility:

> The burgher is for that reason essentially a creature of weak instincts, anxious, fearful of giving of himself, easy to rule. For this reason he has substituted for power the voice of the majority . . . for responsibility, the vote. (IV, 237)

Since he has little vitality (*Lebensintensität*), the burgher anxiously seeks to effect a compromise between nature and spirit in order to save his identity (IV, 237). The ironic description of the burgher's fearful attempts to secure peace and security "in a mild and healthful zone without violent storms and showers" (IV, 237) is reminiscent of the ironic portrayal of the "last man" in *Thus Spake Zarathustra*.

The security and very existence of the burgher depends on the vitality of certain "outsiders." These are lonely individuals, "strong and wild personalities" who detest law, virtue and "common sense" (IV, 237). The stronger among them "break through the atmosphere of the bourgeois earth and soar into the cosmic . . . achieve the absolute and go to their destruction in a way to be admired . . ." (IV, 239). The road of these true geniuses is that of *amor fati* and leads as in *Demian* to the terrible loneliness of Jesus in the Garden of Gethsemane. Mozart is lauded as a suffering genius of this sort because of the

> greatness of his dedication and willingness to suffer, because of his indifference to the ideas of the burghers and to that state of extreme isolation which thins the bourgeois air surrounding the suffering one, the one aspiring to true humanity, to icy ether, that state of isolation in the Garden of Gethsemane. (IV, 248)

The "remaining outsiders," who number in the thousands but represent only a small fraction of mankind, are inspired individuals who would like to heed their inner voice and obey the law of *amor fati*, but who cannot bring themselves to spurn such aspects of bourgeois society as cleanliness, order, sociability and art. They suffer from a split-personality and are at one and the same time burgher and outsider, half-man and half-wolf.

Harry Haller is such an individual on the fringe of bourgeois existence—a wolf of the steppes. He embodies that which is "free, wild, untamable, dangerous and strong," yet he is also attracted to the music of Mozart and to human idealism (IV, 227). He feels an inner compulsion to become either saint or sinner and in his freedom from convention he is prepared to love the criminal, the revolutionary and the sophist as if they were his own brother; but his bourgeois upbringing prevents him from feeling more than pity for the common thief and sex-murderer (IV, 236). He is confronted with the weighty decision of whether to venture the "leap into the Absolute" to join the immortals or, with the help of humor, to come to terms with the bourgeois world (IV, 240).

The novel thus deals with a kind of Nietzschean superman who abhors bourgeois superficiality but who cannot bring himself to tread the path of icy isolation of the genius. The author tells us that at issue is the "regal man" and not the little man with whom political science and statistics is concerned, who may be found by the millions on the streets (IV, 250).

In a few instances Hesse reinforces a given theme by referring specifically to Nietzsche. When Haller refuses to go the lonely way of the genius "which would lead me into atmospheric regions where the air grows ever thinner," he links his own feeling of utter isolation with the symbol of stark loneliness in Nietzsche's poem "Vereinsamt":—smoke slowly losing itself in a bleak, wintry sky. The reference is particularly fitting as Nietzsche's obviously autobiographical poem also deals with the outsider whose feeling of growing isolation awakens in him an almost uncontrollable desire to return to the security and warmth of bourgeois society. It is interesting to note that Nietzsche frequently associated the notion of icy-cold with the tragic life-view in order to emphasize the isolation of the individual engaged in the pursuit of such knowledge. Hesse seems to have had a similar idea in mind when he banned the immortals in *Steppenwolf* "to the ice of outer space through which the stars shine" (IV, 407). In the quiet words of Hesse's Mozart the notion of cold is linked with the tragically sublime:

> Cool and without motion is our eternal being,
> Cool and starry bright our eternal laughter. (IV, 407)

Tragic realization, it was said, derives from suffering; in the affirmation of suffering Nietzsche's name is mentioned twice. The fictional editor of the diary tells the reader "that Haller was a genius in suffering, that he, in conformity with many of Nietzsche's utterances, had developed within himself an inspired, unlimited and terrible capacity to suffer" (IV, 193). Then Haller himself, after reading the comment by Novalis that suffering should be recognized as a sign of human dignity, mentions the philosopher: "Fine! Eighty years before Nietzsche!" (IV, 199).

Nietzsche is referred to also in connection with another basic theme of the novel: Haller and his colleagues suffer greatly because their times have not produced a unified style. Haller makes it clear that here the key to a proper understanding of the story may be found (IV, 205). How closely Haller's reasoning is in line with Nietzsche's may be seen from the following comparison. Among other things, Haller had said:

> Human existence becomes truly painful, a hell, when two cultures or two religions overlap. . . . There are times when a whole generation gets caught between two eras, between two life-styles, so that it loses everything that is commonplace, every custom, every privacy and innocence. (IV, 205–206)

The parallel to the first essay in *Thoughts out of Season* is obvious. To cite a few lines will suffice: "Culture is above all the unity of artistic style in all the vital manifestations of a people . . . the German of our time, however, lives in a chaotic melange of all styles. . . ."[9] Haller is made to appear aware of this parallelism of ideas; in the same context he refers to Nietzsche as the forerunner of the modern outsider:

> Naturally, not everyone feels this to the same degree. A sensitive person like Nietzsche had to experience present-day misery a generation ahead of his time—the suffering he had to undergo, lonely and misunderstood, thousands experience today. (IV, 206)

These comments reveal clearly once again, how closely Haller-Hesse, "the pathologic hermit" (IV, 235), identified himself with Nietzsche.

Two further scenes freighted with symbolic import show Nietzschean inspiration. The first of these describes man as a narrow bridge between nature and spirit:

> Man is by no means a firm and durable configuration (this was the ideal of antiquity despite the contrary premonitions of its sages), he is rather an experiment and a transition, he is nothing more than the narrow bridge between nature and spirit. (IV, 247)

These lines not only paraphrase Nietzsche's famous saying, "Man is a rope stretched between the animal and the superman," they also hint at Nietzsche's overthrow of the conventional view of Greek antiquity.

The carnival may be understood as a symbol of the dionysiac intoxication and self-forgetfulness which presage the suppression of individuation[10] in the "Magic Theater":

> An experience that I had never previously undergone in the fifty years of my life . . . was mine in this ball: the experience of the festival, the intoxication of a celebrating community, the mystery of the immersion of the individual in the crowd, of the *Unio mystica* of joy. (IV, 361–62)

Death and the Lover (*Narziß und Goldmund*, 1930) discards the possibility of bourgeois compromise and concentrates on *amor fati* as the means to achieve mystic unity. In this novel the two poles of human existence are presented as independent individuals, the saint and the sinner, Narziß and Goldmund.

The artist Goldmund is a superior man who in his youth resembles

---

[9] Friedrich Nietzsche, "Unzeitgemäße Betrachtungen," *Werke*, ed. Karl Schlechta (Munich: Carl Hanser Verlag, 1954–56), I, 40.

[10] This idea was developed by Nietzsche in his *Birth of Tragedy* (1872).

Demian and in later years, Klingsor. He has no regard for virtue or law, seduces and murders, as destiny demands. He has the ability of the genius "to give himself completely" (V, 43) and obeys the inner voice which again is characterized as the "call of the mother" (V, 83, 192). Narziß, on the other hand, is Hesse's first truly spiritual protagonist; although he is a bit colorless, there is no doubt that he is meant to be a regal person, an intellectual genius, destined to "lifelong striving for saintliness" (V, 36).

The novel treats the familiar theme: the way to self-realization is also the way to unity. In their striving for unity the friends, who in their symbolism represent the duality of human nature and of all life, feel a deep bond and in the course of time draw ever closer to one another, guided, as it were, by a magical destiny. Thus when Goldmund is asked to do a sketch for the master, he almost involuntarily sketches a likeness of Narziß whom he has not seen for many years. He carried out the task "which his heart had assigned him . . . like a sacrificial ritual" (V, 160). The figure he then carves using the sketch as a guide, becomes the disciple Johannes of a religious group, although it is unknown to Goldmund that Narziß had meanwhile become an abbot and assumed the name of Johannes.

Toward the end of his adventurous life, Goldmund stays for a time near the abbey and attains a sense of inner peace in the beneficial proximity of his disciplined friend. Here he achieves the highest degree of unity possible to him and creates his masterpiece, a soulful Madonna of infinite beauty. Then heeding the inner call to chaos, he resumes his wanderings and goes to an early death. Outwardly disreputable, his life had been inwardly rich and meaningful.

Narziß had felt a similar yearning for his friend. He confessed to the dying Goldmund, "I have loved you, you alone of all mankind" (V, 317). Goldmund had made his life complete in teaching him what the words friend, love and, as Hesse formulated it in a subsequent letter, seduction, really meant (VII, 508).

Unity is of course another way of referring to the mystical totality. Narziß had early recognized that their diverse paths led to the same mystical goal. His words are almost those of Demian: "Don't you know that one of the shortest routes to the life of the saint is the life of the sinner?" (V, 38). In his portrayal of the two friends, Hesse had for the last time presented the world as consisting of two halves, order and chaos, the luminous father-world and the dark mother-world, the Apollonian and the Dionysian. But even here, where he was on the verge of disowning the Dionysian world-view, he showed a decided preference for the dark world of the mother.

This is evident from the fact that the only clear symbol of the totality is the God-Mother; and although both men dedicate themselves to *amor fati* and strive toward unity, it is only Goldmund who hears the call of the mother (V, 64). He always sees her as the symbol of totality. As a child he dreams of her as "mother, madonna and beloved" (V, 65); after completing the Johannes figure he has had a brief vision of the primeval mother with her enigmatic, cruel yet tender smile:

> he saw her smiling over the births, the deaths, the flowers, the rustling fall leaves, smiling over art, smiling over decay.
> Everything was equally important to the primeval mother, her mysterious smile hung like the moon over everything. (V, 186)

In death she comes and brings him peace (V, 322).

Goldmund's *amor fati* had led to a full life but the same does not seem to be quite so true of Narziß. How else can one explain the concerned words of the dying vagabond: "But how will you die Narziß, since you have no mother? Without a mother one cannot love. Without a mother one cannot die" (V, 322). Narziß has no answer to this question. He had long missed the "bloody darknesses" in his spotless world of "order and discipline," and concluded that Goldmund's path was "not only more childlike and human . . . it was ultimately more courageous and greater" (V, 308).

In *Journey to the East* (*Morgenlandfahrt*, 1932), Hesse sharply repudiated Nietzschean irrationalism and forever abandoned the concepts of nature and mother. However, with obviously altered connotations, *amor fati* and the notion of the creative genius remained constituent elements of his outlook.

Hesse's rejection of nature in favor of a world of the spirit receives its formal expression in the resurgence of a surrealistic literary style and the subjective treatment of historical time. The goal of the hero is now depicted as the light world of the orient, the land of the rising sun, the luminous sphere of the spirit. The importance of the spiritual aspect is apparent from the emphasis placed on the temporarily lost "holy pact of the brotherhood" (*der heilige Bundesbrief*) around which the story centers and which symbolizes the mystical aspirations of the great creative spirits of all times.

The brotherhood of wayfarers is related to the elite of creative spirits in *Demian*. The brotherhood consists of artistic supermen from all eras of history, "the strongest (army) in the world" (VI, 35). Few in number, the geniuses are born to rule: "There are few who are born to rule, they remain at their tasks cheerful and healthy. The others, however, who have become masters merely by dint of effort, all end badly" (VI, 28).

Rejection of the dark mother world does not mean that Hesse had drastically changed his way of thinking. It meant rather that he was again oscillating toward the other pole of his dichotomous outlook, that St. Francis was once again taking precedence over Nietzsche, that Hesse's earlier humanism was being preferred to the worship of instinct and Nietzschean immoralism. Thus Leo, the leader of the brotherhood—it will be recalled that one of the six disciples of St. Francis was named Leo—designates service (*Dienst*) as the highest good. Ruling is interpreted as a general guiding of humanity in its development. Strength is viewed as the ability to serve, that is, voluntarily to subordinate oneself. Leo has much in common with Camenzind and Siddhartha, with his message of love.

It is not infrequently asserted that in his last novel, *Magister Ludi* (*Glasperlenspiel*, 1932–1943), Hesse finally managed to reconcile the antithetical elements in his basic outlook. This is true only for his revised outlook after 1930. In *Magister Ludi*, Hesse merely reasserted at greater length the theme he had developed in *Journey to the East* that *Geist*—as in the earlier work, referring to spirituality, creativity and intellectuality—had to be placed in the service of mankind, had to be subordinated to *Dienen*. There is virtually no reference to the true antithesis to *Geist*, the dark Nietzschean world of the mother. *Magister Ludi* is concerned with the opposition of introverted intellectuality and extroverted service. Despite this, Nietzsche left his imprint on the novel.

First of all, Nietzsche's particular explanation of cultural decadence, as resulting from the abuse and subsequent loss of creative vigor, provides the substance of the lengthy introductory chapter and the substratum of the entire narrative. The action is set some 500 years in the future to permit a sufficient historical perspective from which to evaluate the excesses and follies of our age, this superficial age, which the fictional historian Ziegenhals ironically terms the era of the feuilleton (VI, 89). The historian points out that our era was a period of "old age and twilight" (VI, 94), in which the creative springs had dried up; this was manifest in the "desolate mechanization of life, the worsened morals, the decline in religion among the peoples, and the insincerity in art" (VI, 94). The Castalian Order and the Bead Game were created by the small remaining elite of intellectuals to preserve the cultural heritage, at a time when the creative forces were admittedly unable to compete with the achievements of the twentieth century (VI, 98). In this monumental fairy-tale Hesse is saying what Nietzsche had said, that our superficial way of life is hostile to the creation and preservation of true culture, and that we must do something about it before it is too late.

Nietzsche's thought so permeates virtually every nuance of the introductory chapter that it is not surprising to see his name appear several times, breaking, as it were, the surface of Hesse's consciousness. In commenting on the dissipation of the creative forces, the narrator writes:

> One had just discovered (a discovery that had been occasionally anticipated here and there ever since Nietzsche) that youth and the creative spirit were a thing of the past, and that old age and dusk had set in . . . (VI, 94)

Nietzsche is also alluded to as one of the great thinkers of our time, in connection with the narrator's discussion of the unfortunate tendency of the feuilletonistic era to prefer popular and sensational writing about great persons to reading these people in the original. Typical of the sort of thing our generation liked to read was an article entitled "Friedrich Nietzsche and Women's Styles around 1870" (VI, 90), implying that the readers of our century had become too effete to appreciate great cultural contributions such as the weighty and meaningful ideas of Nietzsche.[11]

In the story itself, which follows the conventional format of the apprenticeship novel, the autobiographical hero Josef Knecht resembles the earlier Nietzschean protagonists. Although he ultimately comes to see in service to others the highest good, he is essentially the outsider, the artistic genius, the leader of the "intellectual elite" (VI, 106), who has achieved "the highest conceivable level of accomplishment" (VI, 119). He affirms life in the sense of *amor fati* and resigns himself to existence with dignity, by feeling "without personal rancor the tragedy inherent in every person consecrated to *Geist*" (VI, 117). His selfless devotion to destiny provides the main theme of the novel:

> It is not so much this tragedy itself that has induced us to consider in such detail the personality of Josef Knecht; rather it is the quiet, cheerful, even radiant manner in which he carried out his destiny, his gift, his mission. (VI, 117)

The narrator Ziegenhals characterizes Knecht's dedication as *amor fati* and Daimonion (—Demian!): "Like every significant person he has his *Daimonion* and his *amor fati*, but his *amor fati* reveals itself as free from gloom and fanaticism" (VI, 117). Cheerfully and without hesitation, Knecht

---

[11] It is amazing to note that some three decades earlier, as mentioned above, Hesse had alluded to Nietzsche in an almost identical manner, when exposing the superficiality of the tutor Homburger in *Hay-Moon* (*Heumond*, I, 685).

gives his life when the call of destiny requires the ultimate sacrifice.

Not only does Nietzsche provide the thematic substratum of *Magister Ludi*, not only is his name mentioned, not only are Nietzschean motifs in evidence, Nietzsche himself is surprisingly introduced into the action as a flesh-and-blood character, as an associate of Knecht, who symbolizes one of the two main tendencies of the times. These two tendencies, which according to the narrator dominated our culture since the Middle Ages, are as follows:

> the freeing of thought and faith from every sort of authoritative domina-
> tion, i.e., the battle of Reason which had become sovereign and of age
> against the rule of the Roman Catholic Church, and—on the other hand—
> the secret, but passionate search for a legitimation of this freedom, for a new
> and adequate authority coming from within itself. (VI, 88)

The legitimation of human freedom becomes the task of the Benedictine monk, Pater Jakobus, in whom one readily recognizes the famed Swiss historian Jacob Burckhardt. The freeing of thought and faith from every sort of authoritative domination is left to the irresponsible but brilliant glassbead-player Fritz Tegularius. The latter is none other than Friedrich Nietzsche himself.

This identification is easy to substantiate as Tegularius corresponds in every respect to the picture Hesse repeatedly drew of Nietzsche. A few pertinent phrases to indicate the correspondence will suffice (VI, 365–68):

Tegularius is affectionately referred to as "this Fritz," the familiar form of Nietzsche's Christian name. He was pathologically sick, "one who was ill throughout his entire life"; "that which one called his sickness was ultimately and predominantly . . . a completely individualistic attitude and way of life." "He was basically incurable, as he didn't really want to be cured." Knecht was interested in him not only because of his talent and erroneous views but also because of this "sickness."

Tegularius was an artist and a genius: "the sublime artist of the glass-bead game, his extraordinary talent, his restless geniality ever receptive to the problems of the glassbead game"; "his precious gifts, his melancholy genius, his temperamental artistic passion." He was in spirit an aristocrat: "not an average person, he was an aristocrat, a very highly talented person."

He was an outsider who had no regard for conventional views: ". . . he loved nothing but his freedom, his eternal student-outlook, he preferred to remain his life long the sickly, incalculable and stubborn individualist."

He was a pessimist and nihilist: "where his pessimistic wit sparkled and no one could resist the gloomy splendor of his views"; "the inspired jester and nihilist." Although he was an incomparable genius who inspired his own time favorably, he was decadent and a danger for later generations: "It was marvelous and delightful that this Fritz had lived. But the dissolution of Castalia into a dreamland populated by nothing but Tegulariusses had to be prevented." Tegularius also shares Nietzsche's views, although Hesse simplified these somewhat, just as he had simplified the views of Burckhardt, to adapt to the simplified thesis of his novel: individual versus society. Accordingly, the keen-witted glassbead-player rejects any "concern for history," and considers history itself as unworthy of study (VI, 374). Just as Nietzsche had done in his second essay in *Thoughts out of Season*, Tegularius admits that "the interpretation of history, the philosophy of history, can be carried on in a witty amusing, possibly even highly pathetic manner," (VI, 374) but he disdains history *per se*:

> But the thing itself, the object of this humor, namely history, was something so hateful, at the same time so banal and devilish, so coarse and boring, that he did not understand how anyone could occupy himself with it.

He is an advocate of "un-historicity and over-historicity," and praises the "absolutely unhistorical and contra-historical which is divine and freed from time."

Hesse playfully wove a few further Nietzschean phrases into Tegularius' discourse such as "the exploitation of the weak through the strong," "the self-glorifying battle for power which is eternally the same, eternally self-overcoming," and a reference to religion and art as "illusory façades."

The most significant statement for this investigation is, of course, the admission by Knecht cited earlier that Tegularius had played a critical role in his life as an inspiring force:

> We are of the opinion that in Knecht's life this Tegularius was no less necessary and important than Designori and the Pater in Marienfels, and to be sure in the same way, as an inspirational force, as an open window to new viewpoints. (VI, 367)

And, as we have said, since Designori shared the views of the Pater, it is evident that in the opinion of the old and carefully deliberating Hesse, Nietzsche and Burckhardt had provided him with the most significant intellectual stimulation.[12]

[12] A bit further on in the story, Knecht restricts the importance of Tegularius to "polishing and minor details" whereas he, Knecht, was responsible for the "basic structure and direction" as well as "the meditation sequence" (VI, 369–70). Evidently Hesse on

One cannot terminate this discussion without commenting on the unusual parallelism between Hesse's *Magister Ludi* and Thomas Mann's *Dr. Faustus* (1947). Both of these monumental novels evaluating Germany and Europe in the Hitler era and war years accomplished the following:

1) they disowned Nietzsche and declared him dangerous
2) they used him as a central figure to symbolize the threat he proved
3) they utilized the problem of creative vigor in the face of decadence as their basic substratum
4) they admitted Nietzsche's genius.

★   ★   ★

Following this brief survey of Hesse's principal writings, we would now like to summarize our findings. It would appear that Nietzsche had virtually no effect on the transcendental base of Hesse's outlook. This base is the product of Hesse's pietistic upbringing and of the great mystical teachings of East and West. Nevertheless, one cannot disregard Nietzsche's contribution to Hesse's thought as inconsequential. We hope to have shown that Hesse received definite inspiration from Nietzsche with respect to:

1) his conviction that bourgeois culture was decadent
2) his division of mankind into the strong and the weak
3) his ideal of a superhuman genius
4) his conception of pathologic modern man
5) his belief in the cultural mission of the inspired individual
6) his acceptance of the notion of *amor fati*.

It is conceivable that many of Hesse's stylistic experiments as well as his antirationalism may be traced back, at least in part, to Nietzsche.

All this is important. Furthermore, we have attempted to show that Nietzsche, interpreted by Hesse as a nihilist, reinforced the nihilistic doubts of the wavering author. This is as evident in *Hermann Lauscher* as it is in *Magister Ludi*, where Burckhardt as the Pater represented "faith and order" (VI, 252), and the "jester and nihilist" Nietzsche symbolized the counter-pole of chaos and disbelief.

second thought wanted to make it clear that his basic viewpoint was truly his own. Although this cannot be disputed, "polishing and minor details" does not do full justice to Hesse's earlier statements that no writer other than Goethe had caused him to ponder life as had Nietzsche.

One need only to reflect for a moment on the frequency with which Hesse's heroes are forced to combat nihilism, how often they stand on the brink of despair and how often many of them succumb. The inveterate nihilists Lauscher and Muoth commit suicide. Klein regains faith only at the moment he takes his life. Siddhartha barely rescues himself after attempting suicide. The Steppenwolf calls himself a suicidal type and wanders from one torment to the next. Heilner and Camenzind achieve a limited affirmation only with great effort. Demian's path is termed a "route for desperate individuals" (VII, 519). The resort guest in the story of the same name has the bitter taste of despair on his tongue. Goldmund temporarily loses his faith in the world and in God and, as he once said, seeks to forget the horror and chaos in sensual joy. In similar fashion, despairing H.H. temporarily loses faith in the ideals of the East; "nowhere," he cries, "is there a unity, a center, a point around which the wheel turns" (VI, 35).

It would not be correct to label Hesse a nihilist. Without doubt he did everything in his power to affirm his transcendental ideal. But it was not an easy task. Even though his heroes usually won out, they always had a long and bitter fight, and each time the battle had to be fought anew. Each time the goal was a bit different, too, a clear indication that the previous victory had not been quite what he had hoped it would be. In 1932 Hesse wrote:

And whenever I think that I have expressed my faith in a suitable form, it soon appears dubious and foolish, and I am compelled to seek anew for confirmations and other forms. At times this is torment and distress, at other times it is bliss. (VII, 527)

We have already cited the letter written in 1931 in which Hesse virtually admitted that faith and nihilism were the two poles of his existence (VII, 509). We therefore feel justified in viewing Nietzsche as the great antagonist in Hesse's life, with whom the writer, according to his own statement, had to wrestle again and again. In the concepts of the genius and *amor fati* Nietzsche offered encouragement and a way out of the dilemma, but on other occasions his nihilism gravely reinforced Hesse's despair.

In a word, Hesse's life was a constant battle with Nietzschean nihilism. Like so many of his famous literary contemporaries—Hauptmann, Musil, Broch, Rilke, George, Kaiser, Morgenstern, to mention a few—Hesse sought to bridge this abyss with a personal mysticism, for many years with only partial success.

THE WRITINGS OF HERBERT W. REICHERT

The Writings of Herbert W. Reichert

A. Books

1949   1. *Basic Concepts in the Philosophy of Gottfried Keller*. UNC Studies in the Germanic Languages and Literatures, No. 1. Chapel Hill: The University of North Carolina Press, 1949. 164 pp.

       1a. Reprint. New York: AMS Press, 1966.

1959   2. (Ed.). *Deutsche Hörspiele. Four German Radio Plays*. New York: Appleton-Century-Crofts, 1959. 266 pp.

1960   3. (Ed. with Karl Schlechta). *International Nietzsche Bibliography*. UNC Studies in Comparative Literature, No. 29. Chapel Hill: The University of North Carolina Press, 1960. 150 pp.

       3a. Rev. and expanded ed. UNC Studies in Comparative Literature, No. 45. Chapel Hill: The University of North Carolina Press, 1968. 180 pp. [Cf. also B/30 and B/32.]

1963   4. (Ed. with Herman Salinger). *Studies in Arthur Schnitzler*. UNC Studies in the Germanic Languages and Literatures, No. 42. Chapel Hill: The University of North Carolina Press, 1963. 120 pp.

       4a. Reprint. New York: AMS Press, 1966.

1968   5. (Trans.). *Friedrich Nietzsche: His Personality and His Philosophy* by Ola Hansson. Mount Pleasant, Michigan: The Enigma Press, 1968. 35 pp.

1972   6. *The Impact of Nietzsche on Hermann Hesse*. Mount Pleasant, Michigan: The Enigma Press, 1972. 93 pp. [Expanded version of B/26.]

B. Articles

1946   1. "Gottfried Keller's Conception of Freedom," *Monatshefte*, 38 (1946), 65–82.

1947　2. "A Comparison of the Philosophies of Schiller and Keller," *Monatshefte*, 39 (1947), 170–77.

1948　3. "Translation and the Reading Objective," *German Quarterly*, 21 (1948), 175–84.

1949　4. "The Philosophy of Archytas in Wieland's *Agathon*," *Germanic Review*, 24 (1949), 8–17.

　　　5. "Goethe's *Faust* in Two Novels by Thomas Mann," *Factotum*, 3 (May 1949), 23–27.

　　5a. *German Quarterly*, 22 (1949), 209–14.

　　　6. "The Characterization of Bancbanus in Grillparzer's *Ein treuer Diener seines Herrn*," *Studies in Philology*, 46 (1949), 70–78.

1950　7. "Gottfried Keller's Conservative Attitude toward the Revolution of 1848," *The Swiss Record*, 2 (1950), 73–80.

1955　8. "Some Causes of the Nestroy Renaissance," *Monatshefte*, 47 (1955), 221–30.

　　　9. "A Travesty on Franz Werfel's *Spiegelmensch*," *South Atlantic Bulletin*, 20/3 (1955), 12. [Abstract.]

1956　10. "Hints on Producing a Foreign Language Play," *German Quarterly*, 29 (1956), 124–30.

　　　11. "As Others See Us," *Kentucky Foreign Language Quarterly*, 3 (1956), 129–35.

　　　12. "Caricature in Keller's *Der Grüne Heinrich*," *Monatshefte*, 48 (1956), 371–79.

　　　13. "A Comment on Victor J. Lemke's 'The Deification of Gottfried Keller,' " *Monatshefte*, 48 (1956), 380–82.

1957　14. "The Feud between Franz Werfel and Karl Kraus," *Kentucky Foreign Language Quarterly*, 4 (1957), 146–50.

1959　15. "Conventional Textbooks in the Foreign-Language Telecourse," *German Quarterly*, 32 (1959), 34–42.

　　　16. "The Present Status of Nietzsche: Nietzsche Literature in the Post-War Era," *Monatshefte*, 51 (1959), 103–20.

1961　17. "Hauptmann's *Frau Wolff* and Brecht's *Mutter Courage*," *German Quarterly*, 34 (1961), 439–48.

17a. [German translation by Wulf Küster.] "Hauptmanns Frau Wolff und Brechts Mutter Courage," *Gerhart Hauptmann*, ed. Hans-Joachim Schrimpf. Wege der Forschung, vol. 207. Darmstadt: Wissenschaftliche Buchgesellschaft. [1976 (?)].

1963   18. "Nietzsche and Schnitzler," *Studies in Arthur Schnitzler* [Cf. A/4 and A/4a], pp. 95–107.

19. "Arthur Schnitzler and Modern Ethics," *Journal of the International Arthur Schnitzler Research Association*, 2/1 (1963), 21–24.

1964   20. "Nietzsche and Georg Kaiser," *Studies in Philology*, 61 (1964), 85–108.

1965   21. "Schnitzlers egoistische Künstlergestalten," *Journal of the International Arthur Schnitzler Research Association*, 4/2 (1965), 20–27.

1966   22. "German Literature," *The New Book of Knowledge*. New York: Grolier, 1966, VII, 174–81.

23. "Nietzschean Influence in Musil's *Der Mann ohne Eigenschaften*," *German Quarterly*, 39 (1966), 12–29.

24. "Schnitzler and *Jung-Wien*," *Journal of the International Arthur Schnitzler Research Association*, 5/3 (1966), 27–32.

1967   25. "Friedrich Nietzsche," *Encyclopedia of World Literature in the 20th Century*. New York: Frederick Ungar, 1967, II, 449–52.

26. "Nietzsche et Hermann Hesse. Un Example d'Influence," *Nietzsche*. Paris: Editions de Minuit, 1967, pp. 153–67. [Cf. also A/6.]

1970   27. "Symbolism in Gottfried Keller's *Sinngedicht*," *Studies in German Literature of the Nineteenth and Twentieth Centuries. Festschrift for Frederic E. Coenen*, ed. Siegfried Mews. UNC Studies in the Germanic Languages and Literatures, No. 67. Chapel Hill: The University of North Carolina Press, 1970, pp. 111–25. 2nd ed. 1972.

1972   28. "Nietzsche und Carl Sternheim," *Nietzsche Studien*, 1 (1972), 334–52.

29. "Nietzsche in the Sixties," *Malahat Review*, 24 (1972), 103–20.

1973   30. "International Nietzsche Bibliography 1968–1972," *Nietzsche Studien*, 2 (1973), 320–39.

31. "The Ethical Import of the Artist in the Works of Arthur Schnitzler," *Modern Austrian Literature*, 6/1–2 (1973), 123–50.

31a. *Ethos und Verantwortung im Werk Arthur Schnitzlers*, ed. Manfred Kuxdorf. Bern and Frankfurt am Main: Lang, [1975 (?)].

32. "International Nietzsche Bibliography 1972–1973," *Nietzsche Studien*, 4 (1975), 351–73.

C. Reviews

1954   1. *Deutsche Verse: Gedichte, Reime und Sprüche als Weg zum gesprochenen Deutsch*. I. Teil: *Aus der Jugendzeit* (Chicago, 1951). *German Quarterly*, 27 (1954), 272–74.

1956   2. *Amphitryon in Frankreich und Deutschland* by Hansres Jacobi (Zurich, 1952). *Comparative Literature*, 8 (1956), 354–55.

3. *Georg Christoph Lichtenberg, précurseur du romantisme. L'homme et l'oeuvre* by H. Schöffler (Nancy, 1954). *Modern Language Notes*, 71 (1956), 621–23.

4. *Die lyrischen Vorstufen des "Grünen Heinrich"* by Alexander Dürst (Bern, 1955). *Monatshefte*, 48 (1956), 104–5.

1960   5. Friedrich Nietzsche. *Unpublished Letters*, trans. Kurt F. Leidecker (New York, 1959). *News and Observer* (Raleigh, N. C., 10 Jan. 1960), Section 3, p. 6.

6. *Die Struktur des epischen Theaters. Dramaturgie der Kontraste* by Herbert Crumbach (Braunschweig, 1960). *Modern Language Notes*, 79 (1960), 477–79.

7. Gottfried Keller, *Sämtliche Werke in acht Bänden*, ed. Peter Goldammer (Berlin, 1958). *Journal of English and German Philology*, 59 (1960), 371–72.

8. *The Mind of Germany* by Hans Kohn (New York, 1960). *News and Observer* (Raleigh, N. C., 8 May 1960), Section 3, p. 5.

1961   9. *Frisch und Dürrenmatt* by Hans Bänziger (Bern and Munich, 1960). *Journal of English and Germanic Philology*, 60 (1961), 537–38.

10. *Gottfried Kellers Martin Salander. Untersuchungen zur Struktur des Zeitromans* by Margarete Merkel-Nipperdey (Göttingen, 1959). *Journal of English and Germanic Philology*, 60 (1961), 532–34.

1963   11. *Essays in German and Comparative Literature* by Oskar Seidlin (Chapel Hill, 1961), *Comparative Literature*, 15 (1963), 65–67.

12. *Deutsche Literatur der Gegenwart* by Walter Jens (Munich, 1961). *German Quarterly*, 36 (1963), 303–4.

1964   13. *Ein voller Erdentag. Gerhart Hauptmann: Werk und Gestalt* by Carl Zuckmayer (Frankfurt am Main, 1962). *German Quarterly*, 37 (1964), 174–75.

1965   14. *Nietzsche in der Hispania* by Udo Rukser (Bern, 1962). *Modern Language Notes*, 81 (1965), 284–85.

15. *Spiegel und Echo. Fünf deutsche Hörspiele*, ed. Frederick G. Goldberg (New York, 1965). *Modern Language Journal*, 49 (1965), 510–11.

1966   16. Gottfried Keller, *Galatea Legenden (Sieben Legenden im Urtext)*, ed. Karl Reichert (Frankfurt am Main, 1965). *German Quarterly*, 39 (1966), 643–44.

17. *Leibniz. Allbeseelung und Skepsis* by Hans M. Wolff (Bern, 1961). *Modern Language Notes*, 81 (1966), 650–52.

18. *Der Briefwechsel zwischen Gottfried Keller und Hermann Hettner*, ed. Jürgen Jahn (Berlin, 1964). *German Quarterly*, 39 (1966), 641–42.

1967   19. *Der Realismus in der schweizerischen Literatur* by Karl Fehr (Bern and Munich, 1965). *Journal of English and German Philology*, 66 (1967), 429–31.

20. *Literatursoziologische Studien zu Gottfried Kellers Dichtung* by Michael Kaiser (Bonn, 1965). *German Quarterly*, 40 (1967), 720–21.

1968   21. *Friedrich Nietzsche* by Peter Pütz (Stuttgart, 1967). *Journal of English and Germanic Philology*, 68 (1968), 129–30.

22. *Modern German Literature. The Figures in Context* by Henry Hatfield (New York, 1967). *Modern Language Journal*, 52 (1968), 42–43.

1969   23. *The Sleepwalkers. Elucidation of Hermann Broch's Trilogy* by Dorrit C. Cohn (The Hague, 1966). *Monatshefte*, 61 (1969), 86–87.

1970   24. *Hermann Broch. Der Dichter und seine Zeit* by Manfred Durzak (Stuttgart, 1968). *Monatshefte*, 62 (1970), 168–70.

25. *Briefwechsel über Literatur* by Helmut Heissenbüttel and Heinrich Vormweg (Berlin, 1969). *Books Abroad*, 44 (1970), 467–68.

26. Walter Benjamin, *Illuminations*, trans. Harry Zohn (New York, 1969). *Monatshefte*, 62 (1970), 409–10.

27. *Gottfried Kellers Sinngedicht* by Ernst May (Bern, 1969). *Journal of English and Germanic Philology*, 62 (1970), 368–71.

28. *Gottfried Keller. Der Weg zur Reife* by Kaspar Locher (Bern and Munich, 1969). *Monatshefte*, 62 (1970), 388–89.

1971   29. *Nietzsche in England: 1890–1914. The Growth of a Reputation* by David S. Thatcher (Toronto, 1970). *Journal of English and Germanic Philology*, 70 (1971), 522–24.

30. *Wirklichkeit und Kunst in Gottfried Kellers Roman "Der Grüne Heinrich"* by Hartmut Laufhütte (Bonn, 1969). *Monatshefte*, 63 (1971), 186–88.

31. *Dichter über ihre Dichtungen: Gottfried Keller*, ed. Klaus Jeziorkowski (Munich, 1970). *Monatshefte*, 63 (1971), 73–74.

1972   32. Martin Heidegger, *Poetry, Language, Thought*, trans. Albert Hofstadter (New York, 1971). *Books Abroad*, 46 (1972), 670–71.

33. *Artistic Consciousness and Political Conscience. The Novels of Heinrich Mann 1900–1938* by David Roberts (Bern and Frankfurt am Main, 1971). *Monatshefte*, 64 (1972), 300–2.

34. *Naturalismus und Symbolismus im Frühwerk Thomas Manns* by Christopher Geiser (Bern, 1971). *Monatshefte*, 64 (1972), 298–99.

35. *Thomas Mann. A Critical Study* by R. J. Hollingdale (Lewisburg, 1971). *Monatshefte*, 64 (1972), 288–91.

36. *Nietzsche. Seine Philosophie der Gegensätze und die Gegensätze seiner Philosophie* by Wolfgang Müller-Lauter (Berlin, 1971). *Monatshefte*, 64 (1972), 181–83.

37. *Nietzsches Werke. Kritische Gesamtausgabe*, 30 vols. in 8 sections, ed. Giorgio Colli and Mazzino Montinari (Berlin and New York, 1967 ff.). *Monatshefte*, 64 (1972), 183–84.

1973   37a. [Expanded version.] *Journal of the History of Philosophy*, 11 (1973), 128–30.

38. *The Challenge of German Literature*, ed. Horst Daemmrich and Diether Haenicke (Detroit, 1971). *German Quarterly*, 46 (1973), 465–67.

39. *Thomas Mann: Profile and Perspectives* by André von Gronicka (New York, 1970). *Monatshefte*, 65 (1973), 205–6.

40. *Friedrich Nietzsche. Von den verborgenen Anfängen seines Philosophierens* by Karl Schlechta and Anni Anders (Stuttgart, 1962). *Nietzsche Studien*, 2 (1973), 313–14.

41. *Säkularisation und neue Heiligkeit. Religiöse und religionsbezogene Sprache bei Friedrich Nietzsche* by Manfred Kaempfert (Berlin, 1971). *Journal of English and Germanic Philology*, 72 (1973), 419–20.

1974   42. *Nietzsche: Disciple of Dionysus* by Rose Pfeffer (Lewisburg, 1972). *Monatshefte*, 66 (1974), 176–78.

1975   43. *Heinrich Mann. Dichter und Moralist* by Hanno König (Tübingen, 1972). *Monatshefte*, 67 (1975), 92–94.

[Scheduled for publication]

44. *Die Stellung Nietzsches in der Entwicklung der modernen Literaturwissenschaft* by Elrud Kunne-Ibsch (Tübingen, 1972). *Colloquia Germanica*.

45. *Die Farben und ihre Bedeutung im dichterischen Werk Gottfried Kellers* by Esther Straub-Fischer (Bern, 1972). *Colloquia Germanica*.

46. *Hesse. A Collection of Critical Essays*, ed. Theodore Ziolkowski (Englewood Cliffs, N. J., 1973). *German Quarterly*.

D. Free Adaptations of German "Ribald" Classics
(published under pseudonyms)

1. "The Rabbit and the Turtle Dove," trans. William H. Schad. *Playboy*, 4/10 (October 1957), 5, 9, 80.

1a. Reprinted in: *Playboy's Ribald Classics*. Chicago: Playboy Press, 1966, pp. 143–47.

2. "An Initial Investment," trans. William H. Schad. *Playboy*, 5/2 (February 1958), 67–68.

3. "Fabliau of the Imprisoned Bride," trans. T. E. Bull. *Rogue*, 3/7 (September 1958), 23, 24, 68, 69.

4. "The Undoing of Aristotle," trans. William H. Schad. *Playboy*, 6/6 (June 1959), 65–66.

5. "The Burger's Beautiful Wife," by Johannes von Freiberg, trans. William H. Schad. *Playboy*, 7/1 (January 1960), 59.

5a. Reprinted in: *More Playboy's Ribald Classics*. Chicago: Playboy Press, 1969, pp. 177–79.

6. "A Sackful of Truths—and Surprises," trans. William H. Schad. *Playboy* 10/4 (April 1963), 123–26.

6a. Reprinted in *Playboy's Ribald Classics*. Chicago: Playboy Press, 1966, pp. 124–31.

UNIVERSITY OF NORTH CAROLINA
STUDIES IN THE GERMANIC LANGUAGES
AND LITERATURES

For other volumes in the "Studies" see page ii and following pages.

Send orders to: (U.S. and Canada)
The University of North Carolina Press, P.O. Box 2288
Chapel Hill, N.C. 27514
(All other countries) Feffer and Simons, Inc., 31 Union Square, New York, N.Y. 10003

UNIVERSITY OF NORTH CAROLINA
STUDIES IN THE GERMANIC LANGUAGES
AND LITERATURES

Initiated by RICHARD JENTE (1949–1952), *established by* F. E. COENEN (1952–1968)

Publication Committee

SIEGFRIED MEWS, EDITOR   JOHN G. KUNSTMANN   GEORGE S. LANE

HERBERT W. REICHERT   CHRISTOPH E. SCHWEITZER   SIDNEY R. SMITH

1. Herbert W. Reichert. THE BASIC CONCEPTS IN THE PHILOSOPHY OF GOTTFRIED KELLER. 1949. Reprint.
2. Olga Marx and Ernest Morwitz. THE WORKS OF STEFAN GEORGE. Rendered into English. 1949. Reprint. (See volume 78.)
3. Paul H. Curts. HEROD AND MARIAMNE. A Tragedy in Five Acts by Friedrich Hebbel. Translated into English Verse. 1950. Reprint.
4. Frederic E. Coenen. FRANZ GRILLPARZER'S PORTRAITURE OF MEN. 1951. Reprint.
5. Edwin H. Zeydel and B. Q. Morgan. THE PARZIVAL OF WOLFRAM VON ESCHENBACH. Translated into English Verse, with Introductions, Notes, and Connecting Summaries. 1951, 1956, 1960. Reprint.
6. James C. O'Flaherty. UNITY AND LANGUAGE: A STUDY IN THE PHILOSOPHY OF JOHANN GEORG HAMANN. 1952. Reprint.
7. Sten G. Flygt. FRIEDRICH HEBBEL'S CONCEPTION OF MOVEMENT IN THE ABSOLUTE AND IN HISTORY. 1952. Reprint.
8. Richard Kuehnemund. ARMINIUS OR THE RISE OF A NATIONAL SYMBOL. (From Hutten to Grabbe.) 1953. Reprint.
9. Lawrence S. Thompson. WILHELM WAIBLINGER IN ITALY. 1953. Reprint.
10. Frederick Hiebel. NOVALIS, GERMAN POET–EUROPEAN THINKER–CHRISTIAN MYSTIC. 2nd rev. ed. 1959. Reprint.
11. Walter Silz. REALISM AND REALITY: STUDIES IN THE GERMAN NOVELLE OF POETIC REALISM. 4th Printing. 1965. Pp. xiv, 168. Cloth $6.00.
12. Percy Matenko. LUDWIG TIECK AND AMERICA. 1954. Reprint.
13. Wilhelm Dilthey.. THE ESSENCE OF PHILOSOPHY. Rendered into English by Stephen A. Emery and William T. Emery. 1954, 1961. Reprint.
14. Edwin H. Zeydel and B. Q. Morgan. GREGORIUS. A Medieval Oedipus Legend by Hartmann von Aue. Translated in Rhyming Couplets with Introduction and Notes. 1955. Reprint.
15. Alfred G. Steer, Jr. GOETHE'S SOCIAL PHILOSOPHY AS REVEALED IN *CAMPAGNE IN FRANKREICH AND BELAGERUNG VON MAINZ*. With three full-page illustrations. 1955. Reprint.
16. Edwin H. Zeydel. GOETHE THE LYRIST. 100 Poems in New Translations facing the Original Texts. With a Biographical Introduction and an Appendix on Musical Settings. 2nd rev. ed., 1965. Reprint.
17. Hermann J. Weigand. THREE CHAPTERS ON COURTLY LOVE IN ARTHURIAN FRANCE AND GERMANY. 1956. Reprint.
18. George Fenwick Jones. WITTENWILER'S "RING" AND THE ANONYMOUS SCOTS POEM "COLKELBIE SOW." Two Comic-Didactic Works from the Fifteenth Century. Translated into English. With five illustrations. 1956. Reprint.
19. George C. Schoolfield. THE FIGURE OF THE MUSICIAN IN GERMAN LITERATURE. 1956. Reprint.
20. Edwin H. Zeydel. POEMS OF GOETHE. A Sequel to GOETHE THE LYRIST. New Translations facing the Originals. With an Introduction and a List of Musical Settings. 1957. Reprint.
21. Joseph Mileck. HERMANN HESSE AND HIS CRITICS. The Criticism and Bibliography of Half a Century. 1958. Reprint.
22. Ernest N. Kirrmann. DEATH AND THE PLOWMAN or THE BOHEMIAN PLOWMAN. A Disputatious and Consolatory Dialogue about Death from the Year 1400. Translated from the Modern German Version of Alois Bernt. 1958. Reprint.

For other volumes in the "Studies" see preceding and following pages and p. ii.

Order reprinted books from: AMS PRESS, Inc.,
56 East 13th Street, New York, N.Y. 10003

UNIVERSITY OF NORTH CAROLINA
STUDIES IN THE GERMANIC LANGUAGES
AND LITERATURES

Initiated by RICHARD JENTE (1949–1952), *established by* F. E. COENEN (1952–1968)

Publication Committee

SIEGFRIED MEWS, EDITOR   JOHN G. KUNSTMANN   GEORGE S. LANE

HERBERT W. REICHERT   CHRISTOPH E. SCHWEITZER   SIDNEY R. SMITH

For other volumes in the "Studies" see preceding pages and p. ii.

Order reprinted books from: AMS PRESS, Inc.,
56 East 13th Street, New York, N.Y. 10003

F3